Prophet on the Payroll

When Pulpit and Pew Clash

by

John R. Bodo

Ragged Edge Press

This Ragged Edge Press publication
was printed by
Beidel Printing House, Inc.
63 West Burd Street
Shippensburg, PA 17257-0152 USA

In respect for the scholarship contained herein, the acid-free paper used in this book meets the guidelines for permanence and durability of the Committee on Production Guidelines for Book Longevity of the Council on Library Resources.

For a complete list of available publications
please write
Ragged Edge Press
Division of White Mane Publishing Company, Inc.
P.O. Box 152
Shippensburg, PA 17257-0152 USA

Library of Congress Cataloging-in-Publication Data

Bodo, John R.
Prophet on the payroll : when pulpit and pew clash / by John R. Bodo.
p. cm.
ISBN 1-57249-156-6 (pbk. : alk. paper)
1. Christianity and politics--Sermons. 2. Presbyterian Church--Sermons. 3. Sermons, American. I. Title.
BR115.P7B6534 1999
252'.051--dc21 98-46475
CIP

PRINTED IN THE UNITED STATES OF AMERICA

CONTENTS

PROLOGUE

Prophets in the Bible come in two kinds: true and false. Both claim to have "a word from the Lord," to be privy to God's will. Both proclaim God's will as they see it and exhort God's people to obey it. And both address public issues rather than only personal and interpersonal problems..

True prophets are dissatisfied with things as they are. They are convinced, for example, that God is fed up with the rich getting richer and the poor poorer. According to their vision, God demands and expects change, for the sake of his beloved poor. A true prophet perceives himself, and often risks his life, as God's social change agent, speaking truth to power in God's name.

False prophets have no quarrel with things as they are. Their words delight the powerful: the political, economic, social elite. Their interpretation of God's will keeps them safely uncritical of their employers, well-paid chaplains to the status quo.

This book is an autobiography of sorts. I was born and raised in Budapest, Hungary, emigrated to the USA with my parents in the fall of 1940, and was ordained two years later as a minister of the Presbyterian Church, USA. During the next 50-plus years, with nearly 40 of them as a pastor, I tried to be faithful to the prophetic mandate of my task, in and out of the pulpit but especially in the pulpit.

I do not recall at what exact moment I arrived at the fundamental conviction that there is only *one* Gospel, personal *and* social, and that therefore I would be responsible, as a minister of the Gospel to address public issues as well as personal and interpersonal problems. As a boy of Jewish ancestry growing up under Hitler's shadow and aware of what Hitler was doing to Jews and threatening to do to all of Europe, I wondered where the churches of Germany were that Hitler should be able to rise to power with so little opposition from Christians. Yes, the *Barmen Declaration* of 1934 was a brave act for which many leaders of the Confessing Church would pay dearly, but it was too little and too late. Lutheranism, with its rigid division between church and state, had offered Germany's millions of Christians no experience in prophetic protest, least of all preventive prophetic protest..

My search for the basis of Christian social concern took more mature shape when I began my theological studies, in 1938, at the University of Geneva. Having grown up Unitarian, this was my first exposure to Calvin and Calvinism. Calvin lacked humor and burned Michael Servetus, but he both preached and lived his conviction that society, rather than just the individual, should be informed and ordered by the Gospel.

My conversion to "one Gospel, personal *and* social" was completed at Union Seminary, New York, where it was my privilege to major in Christian ethics under Reinhold Niebuhr, graduating in the spring of 1942. The record of Niebuhr's social ministry in Detroit, preserved in his *Leaves from the Notebook of A Tamed Cynic*, lighted a fire in my conscience which, I hope, has not quite gone out. In his *Moral Man and Immoral Society*, I found a solid theological foundation for my concern. By the time I was ordained by the Presbytery of New York, in the fall of 1942, I knew that, in my ministry wherever it might take me, I would always try to understand and to fulfil my responsibility for prophecy, for holding up major (and therefore controversial) public issues to the light which shines from the face of Jesus, the Christ.

Let me offer, in brief outline, the *biblical basis* for my lifelong conviction that the pastoral ministry includes, among its many responsibilities, a prophetic mandate to deal with major public issues—primarily from the pulpit.

God's concern for justice and mercy dominates the *Torah.* The commandment concerning the love of God and neighbor, which Jesus enthrones as the "Summary of the Law," is tucked away in Leviticus 19 among laws defending the rights and livelihood of the poor. Within the Decalogue, God's demand for just social relations is not limited to the Second Table. The law of the Sabbath, a labor law, appears on the First Table. So does the law against idolatry, which indicts all pride of nation, race or class.

The writings of the *Prophets* were primarily sermons directed at social/economic/political conditions that created hardship for the poor, the oppressed, the stranger, and were therefore to be challenged in God's name. Prediction, so often confused with prophecy, was always conditional. If the people would change their ways, God would relent. If they held on to an unjust system, they would be punished. Meanwhile, God cared nothing for the "noise of solemn assemblies." God wanted to "let justice roll down like water and righteousness like a mighty stream. . . ." That, at least, was Amos' vision of God's will for his people.

The *Incarnation* itself contains a major prophetic component. God's bias in favor of the poor, the voiceless, the defenseless is evident in the birth of the

Messiah in a stable, into the family of a carpenter. The Magnificat shows God siding with the poor against the rich. And eventually Jesus, in his first sermon on record, takes Isaiah 61:1–2 for his text and defines the Gospel as "good news to the poor. . . ."

For Christians, *Jesus* was surely more than a prophet. However, the record of his *ministry* reveals him clearly as a prophet within the succession of Amos, Isaiah, Jeremiah and, of course, John the Baptist. While he did not "come to destroy the Law but to fulfill it," he defied the Law when it ignored or denied the rightful needs of persons. Compassion, for Jesus, outranked religious observance. God cared about soul and body rather than just about the soul. The poor need bread. The sick need relief and healing. God cares most about "the least of these. . . ."

Nor dare we forget that *Jesus* was executed as a revolutionary. He was not a Zealot, but he did light a fuse under the whole system by dramatizing, in his *death* as much as in his life, the difference between the standards of God's Kingdom and the system whose standard-bearers, the Sadducees, exploited their own people while prospering cozily under the Roman exploiter. Whatever else Jesus had in mind, his willing death has inspired prophets of nonviolence, nonviolent revolutionaries like Mohandas Gandhi or Martin Luther King.

As for the *Resurrection of Jesus*, it is not only the cornerstone of the Christian hope for life with God beyond death; it is also the true prophet's assurance that evil, condoned or acclaimed by false prophets, will not have the last word. Thanks to God's raising Jesus from death, the Kingdom of God has achieved a decisive victory. God's beachhead on Earth is secure. Christians who love to sing "We *shall* overcome," have every right to sing "We *have* overcome," thanks to him. Ever since the Resurrection, God's Kingdom impinges on this world, exerting pressure for justice, for reconciliation, for mercy, for freedom, for peace. To recognize the presence of the Kingdom and to help sustain the pressure it exerts is the responsibility of Christ's men and women in ministry, especially in congregations, especially from the pulpit.

But carrying out this prophetic mandate is a daunting task. We would be *true* prophets, God's social change agents, but we are expected to function as *false* prophets, because we are on the *payroll* of people whose lives and fortunes are invested in the status quo and who therefore will not welcome, or do not even expect, any critical comment on any public issues from their pastor, least of all from the pulpit!

To be sure, most members of our mostly white, mostly middle class churches are fair-minded. They will defend the pastor's freedom of the pulpit, but they will just as likely advise him/her against getting "controversial," against "mixing religion and politics." Criticism, addressed at those in power on behalf of their victims, invites *conflict*; and conflict, at least over political, social, or economic issues, is between unwelcome and outlawed in the majority of our congregations.

The problem goes to the very heart of the *Gospel.* To put it biblically: we have Good News for Hebrew slaves, but our audience is Pharaoh. Not only that, but as pastors we are employed and salaried by Pharaoh, for whom the Good News is bad news. And since no one is willing to pay and keep paying for bad news, we are in a tight spot.

How can so many of us in the ministry manage to be so well-liked, when our congregations are mostly Pharaoh while the Gospel is intended for the Hebrew slaves? When Jesus commanded us to love our *enemies,* he clearly took it for granted that we would have some! Jesus knew that we cannot stand for the things he stood for, the things he would have us stand for, without incurring opposition, persecution, perhaps literal martyrdom. But Jesus could not foresee that any of his disciples would be serving as contented chaplains to Pharaoh. Or Herod. Or Pilate.

Again, when Paul instructs us to be *agents of reconciliation,* the implication is clear: we are supposed to experience *conflict.* Indeed, we are expected to create conflict, as Paul did, in order to secure the conditions of authentic reconciliation. And the primary condition of authentic reconciliation is that it must occur between free equals. You may fantasize all you want about the lion and the lamb lying down together. The only way you can keep that idyll of reconciliation going is to provide, every other day or so, a fresh lamb!

The problem of the prophet on the payroll is most acute in churches of mainline denominations, like my own Presbyterian Church, USA. Our membership standards are lax. We are broadly inclusive and therefore heterogeneous. There are hardly any major public issues on which churchwide agreement exists. In this respect, congregations of a sectarian type—like Fundamentalist churches or Quaker meetings—find it much easier not just to hear about public issues but to act on them corporately.

Christians in Racial Crisis by Ernest Q. Campbell and Thomas K. Pettigrew (Washington, D.C.: Public Affairs Press, 1959) is a classic of its kind, a textbook on the problems pastors face when dealing with a highly controversial public issue. In Little Rock, Arkansas, in 1957, the issue was race: the integration of the schools. The pastors, whom Campbell and Pettigrew studied, fell into three groups. A minority of committed segregationists "prophecied" with the complete approval of their churches. A much smaller minority of integrationists risked their jobs—and promptly lost them. The majority of the pastors ranged from mildly segregationist to mildly integrationist but favored complying with the "law of the land." They either chose to remain silent or were urged to keep mum—for the sake of the "peace and unity" of the church. One integrationist pastor, advised by his board to let well enough alone or else, wondered: "Am I the shepherd of my flock or its pet lamb?" (op. cit., p. 131)

Frustrated prophets on the payroll, ill-trained for the role of social change agent but ill at ease with the status quo which inflicts so much hardship and injustice on the defenseless, comfort themselves by supporting extensive *social service ministries* through their congregations. The concrete good that is being done by these food pantries, clothing centers, clinics sponsored by churches cannot be overestimated. They may be "just band aids," but when a person is bleeding, you cannot let him/her bleed until the health care system is reformed; you need to come up with a band aid and put it on, now! We shall always need Good Samaritans and organizations embodying their compassion.

But let us play with the story for a moment. Suppose the original Good Samaritan was not a one-time traveler but a commuter between palm-fringed Jericho where he lived and Downtown Jerusalem where he worked. Suppose further that every other day he found another fellow-traveler, beaten and robbed, in that ditch beside the road, and that each time he took care of the victim as courageously and as expensively as he had taken care of the first victim. How long would it be before you stopped calling him the Good Samaritan and renamed him the Dumb Samaritan?

What should he do? Obviously, after taking care of a few victims one at a time, he should get busy organizing a citizens' lobby in Jerusalem, so that the government would create a highway patrol to make that road safe! In other words, while *social service*, ministry to victims, will always be needed and may be properly satisfying to its purveyors, *social action*, changing the system, is required to put a stop to victimizing people. God does not offer us a choice between social service and social action. God expects us to be engaged in *both*. They are inseparately paired, like mercy and justice which they respectively represent. The problem is that our churches regard ministries of mercy as appropriate while they consider ministries of justice, bent on changing the status quo, as inappropriate—for the prophet on the payroll.

The sermons which follow are samples of attempts at responsible prophetic preaching by one pastor over a 40-year period. They offer glimpses of our country's history and of the history of our mainline Protestant churches during the same four decades. They are designed to serve as case studies of this kind of preaching. Each sermon is prefaced by a sketch of the *context* in which it was preached. Each sermon is followed by some *comments* regarding its effect (if any) then, and its relevance (if any) many years later. Reaction to the sermons ranged from apathetic to stormy. In spite of a fair number of storms, however, this lowly prophet managed to stay on the payroll throughout. Was this because I had acquired a certain skill in this kind of preaching? Or was it because I was pulling my punches and playing it safe? You be the judge!

TOLERANCE: VIRTUE OR VICE?

Context: Tolerance: Virtue or Vice?

I preached this sermon in the spring of 1947 at the Wolff Memorial Presbyterian Church of Newark, New Jersey. I was 27, in the third year of a five-year pastorate. My parents and I had immigrated from Hungary just six years earlier. We would not receive our citizenship until the fall of 1947. I was single but was helping to support my parents.

Wolff Memorial Church was my first regular pastoral charge. Founded in 1863 as the Third German Presbyterian Church of Newark, it was located in a blue-collar, ethnically mixed but all-white neighborhood known as the Ironbound Section because of the surrounding railroad tracks or, more popularly, as Down Neck. The church numbered some 350 members, including over 50 men in the Armed Forces. The German language was gone, except in private conversation among old-timers. Unlike during World War I, when the name of the neighborhood's main artery had to be changed from Hamburg Place to Wilson Avenue, prejudice against German-Americans did not seem to be an issue—in spite of Hitler. On the other hand, racism and anti-Semitism were very much present within the congregation, surfacing in racial-ethnic jokes and offhand, unguarded remarks.

People would congratulate themselves on the absence, Down Neck, of any "Negro problem," because all the Blacks lived on the other side of South Street, an impassable border. What Hitler was doing to Europe's Jews was barely known, but no one was anxious to find out more about it. And there was considerable anti-Catholic prejudice, because Protestants Down Neck were a tiny minority overshadowed by giant ethnic-Catholic parishes: Italian, German, Polish, Spanish, Portuguese, and Anglo. We formed a kind of defense league with six other Protestant congregations, but had no contact whatever with any of the Catholic churches. Vatican Two lay nearly two decades in the future.

"Tolerance: Virtue or Vice" was my first attempt to deal with intolerance from the pulpit. During the previous year we had welcomed a rabbi as guest preacher. The Session (Board of Elders) debated at length whether his presence in the pulpit in a service of Christian worship could be justified. On another Sunday, we had the choir of a black Baptist church take over the music. Both were "firsts" for the church. Both were well received; at least no one protested or even grumbled within my hearing.

Beyond my desire to be numbered among the forces opposing bigotry and injustice, I had a special reason for writing this sermon. *The Churchman,* a New York-based Episcopalian magazine, was sponsoring an ongoing "Sermon-of-the-Week" contest. Submissions were supposed to exhibit social concern. I do not remember any of the details except that the editor's name was Guy Emery Shipler.

The sermon, my contest entry, has no single text. Luke 13:22–30 comes closest, but example after example from the ministry of Jesus is offered to illustrate God's generous and often unpredictable inclusiveness in contrast with our narrow exclusiveness. The main point, though, is that tolerance is not enough. We need to move from "live and let live" to "live and help live." An alternative title might be: "Wanted: A Fighting Tolerance!"

TOLERANCE: VIRTUE OR VICE?

By John R. Bodo
Pastor
Wolff Memorial Presbyterian Church
Newark, New Jersey
Spring 1947

The other day, in leafing through the Modern Library's *Anthology of American Negro Literature*, I came across a little poem called "Incident."

Once riding in old Baltimore,
Heart-filled, head-filled with glee,
I saw a Baltimorean
Keep looking straight at me.

Now I was eight and very small,
And he was no whit bigger,
And so I smiled, but he poked out
His tongue, and called me, "Nigger."

I saw the whole of Baltimore
From May until December;
Of all the things that happened there
That's all that I remember.

Fate has seen fit, in this case, to indulge in a little irony. For today that little colored boy, Countee Cullen, is known as one of our finest American poets, whereas the white boy who slighted him is a forgotten man, lost in the grey mist of his slum. Were it not for the man at whom he stuck his tongue out, he would not be remembered at all.

Jesus once told a story about a party, given by a strange unconventional host. It seemed that when the seats around the tables were filled, many people who had been expecting an invitation had been left out in the cold, and many who had never dreamed of being invited had been accommodated. Jesus concludes: "People will come from the east and we sat, and the north and south, and take their places in the Kingdom of God. There are those now who will then be first, and there are those now first who will then be last." (Luke 13:30—Goodspeed)

Such surprises do occur even in this earthly life. We can never be too sure who will laugh last. Experience teaches even the worst of us that it pays to be civil rather than rude, kind rather than brutal—that it is unwise to kick a chained dog because his memory may be longer than we think. There is, among the masses of mankind, a grudging, work-a-day, "live-and-let-live" tolerance. It is based on the instinct of self-preservation. Its motto is the negative Golden Rule, "Don't do to others what you wouldn't want done to you."

But there arise the questions, "Does tolerance of this kind have the moral strength to ensure a lasting peace? Is such a tolerance the answer to our quest for social justice and personal integrity? *Is tolerance enough?"*

WHEN TOLERANCE IS A VIRTUE

Webster defines tolerance as something rather commendable. He says, among others, that "tolerance is the disposition to allow beliefs, practices, or habits differing from one's own."

It is a great art to tolerate anything that is different. Anyone who differs too much from us tends to be irritating or even shocking. Our usual reaction is to fear and reject anyone we do not fully understand—anyone who in his religion, manner of speaking, political beliefs, race, or nationality is different from our own. We live with eyes wide open to our neighbor's faults and ears wide open to disparaging rumors about him. Rare is the man, and blessed is the man, who can boast a wide open mind!

No matter how startling any new acquaintance may be—how dark his skin, how poor his English, or how strange his ideas—the truly tolerant man will try to understand him before condemning him. Perhaps he will remember the words of Heinrich Heine, the great German poet who was never fully accepted by his fellow-countrymen because he was a Jew: "To understand all things is to forgive all things." We may even remember the words of another, far greater poet, "Judge not that ye be not judged."

WHEN TOLERANCE IS A POSE

But most of the time the highest potential of tolerance is not realized. Instead, it becomes a pose, to be struck whenever expedient; a profession of faith without conviction or action. I have in mind certain "catch" phrases bandied about by the ignorant and the intolerant, which reveal them at once for what they are. Let me name some of them.

"*I wouldn't want America to be overrun by foreigners. We always get the scum of Europe.*"

This one crops up whenever immigration is being discussed. After striking a pose of tolerance toward distinguished foreigners like Albert Einstein, the intolerant individual hastily qualifies his statement for fear that the Department Justice might hear him and relax the rules. He likes foreigners, he says, but not too many of them and only the very best, of course!

Why, in the name of common sense, should we sift immigrants so carefully, when in our own nation we allow criminals and morons to raise large families? What is more, there would be no Sons or Daughters of the American Revolution today if once upon a time the American mainland had not been overrun by foreigners!

"I wouldn't want to see any harm done to the Jews. Some of my best friends are Jews."

Sure, Hitler had some very good Jewish friends, too. In *Mein Kampf* he even admits that he could not have lived through the bitter cold of the winter of 1922, had it not been for a Jewish friend who gave him an old overcoat. In Nazi Germany there was hardly a man or woman who did not have at least one good Jewish friend. This friend seemed to be an exception to the rule that all Jews were enemies of the German nation. But the rule held fast; and we all know what happened.

And then, there is the prize cliché—the worst of the lot. Whenever you suggest that Negroes still do not have a fair chance, that they must have equal opportunity to learn and to work, that they are entitled not only to justice in our courts, but to genuine social equality, someone is bound to stop you short by objecting, *"You wouldn't want your daughter to marry a Negro, would you?"*

What kind of an argument is that, anyway? My daughter will marry whomsoever she chooses. The only reason I might discourage her from marrying a Negro is my fear of the punishment which her white friends—even the most "tolerant" ones—would inflict on her for doing it.

WANTED: A FIGHTING TOLERANCE

Tolerance is not enough! It is not enough to make allowances for whatever difference there may be between our fellow-men and ourselves. *It is not enough merely to let them live: we have to help them live.*

In a sense, *Jesus* was the most *intolerant* man who ever walked the earth. His blasts at the self-righteous Pharisees are monuments of righteous intolerance. He was thoroughly intolerant of all sham, but more than tolerant of human weakness. His ministry shows an unparalleled record of success in lifting up people whom society had trampled down, and in laying low others who had climbed to high places over the backs of their neighbors. He never ceased to preach and to teach that *God's scale of values* was different from our own and that in God's Kingdom many who are now last would be first. His attitude toward society's outcasts was not cheap tolerance, but costly helpfulness.

When Jesus met Matthew, the *social outcast*, collecting his crooked gains at the customs table, He could have said to him, "My good man, I don't blame you. You are part of a rotten system, that's all. People despise you, but I, for one, sympathize with you." *That* would have been tolerance. Instead, Jesus said to Matthew, "Follow me!" and the tax collector left everything behind to become a new man.

When Jesus met the woman who was a *moral outcast*, He should not have taken note of her at all. Even the most tolerant men have to watch their reputation. Talking to a prostitute in plain view of everybody was clearly unwise. But Jesus was more than tolerant. He appreciated her foolish gift of perfume—the expression of her desperate quest for forgiveness—so deeply that he pointed her out to his entire company as an example of the beauty of repentance.

When Jesus was called to task for mixing too freely with members of other—despised—races, He told the immortal story of the Samaritan who proved to be more humane than the best members of the Hebrew race. The Samaritan was a *racial outcast*, but Jesus honored him above all others to show that God plays no favorites.

Mere tolerance is not enough. At its best it is a negative virtue. At its worst, a positive vice. We need a *fighting tolerance*. Our world is shrinking rapidly. Every twenty-five years or so we launder it in blood which makes it shrink all the faster. Brotherhood is no longer an ideal or a dream. It is an imperative for survival. Lukewarm, insipid, passive tolerance is inadequate. What we need is a restatement of the message of the prophets and of Jesus in terms of positive, saving helpfulness, in terms of uncompromising brotherhood under God!

"Live and let live!" was the call of Old—
The call of the world when the world was cold—
The call of men when they pulled apart—
The call of the race with a chill on the heart.

But "Live and help live!" is the cry of the New—
The cry of the world with the Dream shining through—
The cry of the Brother World rising to birth—
The cry of the Christ for a comrade-like earth.

(Edwin Markham)

Comment: Tolerance: Virtue or Vice?

I did not know enough to capitalize on any effect the sermon might have had. I never set foot on the other side of South Street. I applauded President Truman's order desegregating the Armed Forces, but I was not ready to do anything about what was so rightly identified as "the most segregated hour of the week"—Sunday, 11 to noon. And it did not even occur to me publicly to admit that, according to Hitler's bookkeeping, my parents and I were Jews. I believe that, had I "come out," Father might have suffered a heart attack, so traumatized was he by what he experienced during the years preceding our emigration. In retrospect, I believe that the congregation of Wolff Memorial Church would have survived the shock and that my entire subsequent ministry might have been enriched. But hindsight wisdom is likely to be foolishness. At the time, I was not even a U.S. citizen. I was too young, too green, too fearful to do anything. Beyond preaching . . .

I did receive a personal reward, however. The sermon won a slot in the "Sermon of the Week" series sponsored by *The Churchman.* A few weeks later, Bennett Cerf, the publisher of Random House, read it, beautifully, over WOR, New York. It even appeared in a book, *Sermons of Goodwill*, edited by Dr. Guy Emery Shipler.

Half a century later, many things about this sermon are bound to strike us as quaint. We no longer talk about "Negroes." Sexist language ("man") is proscribed. It may seem delightfully, comically Victorian to begin and end a sermon with a poem, even though both those poems clearly fit.

It is startling to realize, though, that this sermon, in spite of its dated vocabulary, could still be preached and perhaps should still be preached. Racism, anti-Semitism, religious prejudice are very much alive in our country in spite of great strides in civil rights and the emergence of a substantial black middle class. Together we must "live and help live."

THE CHURCH FACES COMMUNISM

Context: The Church Faces Communism

I preached this sermon on September 20, 1953, at the First (now Nassau) Presbyterian Church of Princeton, New Jersey. I was working on my doctoral dissertation in American religious history at Princeton Theological Seminary for the past two years while guest preaching in various pulpits. In early January 1951, Dr. Frank Sergeant Niles, Pastor of First Church, died suddenly. The Session (Board of Elders) called me as Stated Supply (i.e., interim pastor) to serve for six months. Several months later, at the end of 1951, the congregation called me as pastor—by a badly split vote, 250 to 125. I was off to a trying start. After two years, marked by the exodus of the leading Fundamentalists, I felt sufficiently secure to risk a sermon on the year's hottest subject: McCarthyism.

Princeton is much more than a residential suburb of both New York and Philadelphia: it is a small city with its distinctive history, flourishing culture, and considerable wealth. The church, located on the university campus and with strong, historic ties to the university, included a largely liberal contingent of university and seminary faculty along with a growing number of conservative research scientists and businessmen commuters.

In the congregation, the fight over the use of the *Gospel Light Press* in the Sunday School was over. Its fans had moved out to found a nondenominational church of their own. First Church adopted the new, historical-critical *Faith and Life Curriculum* of the Presbyterian Church, USA. In the Senate, however, Joe McCarthy of Wisconsin was conducting his anti-Communist crusade, ravaging people's reputation and livelihood, driving dozens of his victims to suicide.

In May of 1953, the Presbyterian General Assembly adopted a report courageously critical of the McCarthy witch hunt. I read the report in *Social Progress* magazine and made it available to the members of the Session.

Session authorized me to reprint excerpts from the report in the *First Church Weekly*. At the same time, I advised Session that I was planning to preach on Communism and anti-Communism. There were words of caution, but no resistance, no threats.

In the July 1953 issue of *The American Mercury*, J. B. Matthews, Staff Director of the McCarthy Committee, claimed that "at least seven thousand Protestant ministers" were involved in "the Kremlin conspiracy." While this insane accusation mobilized President Eisenhower, at last, causing McCarthy to fire Matthews, recalling it retrieves the memory of the atmosphere of the second half of 1953. To be sure, the only conspiracy in the churches was a conspiracy of silence about what McCarthy and his cohorts were doing to innocent persons and to the country.

The sermon is based, broadly, on Romans 12:9–21. Verse 21 is the text: "Do not be overcome by evil, but overcome evil with good." I adopted the interpretation of Communism as a "Christian heresy" popularized by President John A. Mackay of Princeton Seminary who, in turn, acknowledged his debt to German philosopher Count Hermann von Keyserling (1880–1946). This approach enabled me to speak appreciatively of Communism's ideals while being properly critical of their betrayal in practice. At the same time, it enabled me to be equally critical of McCarthyism.

THE CHURCH FACES COMMUNISM

By John R. Bodo
Pastor
First (now Nassau) Presbyterian Church
Princeton, New Jersey
September 20, 1953

Some time ago a friend of mine gave me a long lecture about doughnuts. "Doughnuts are bad for you," he said. "They are greasy and indigestible. They are pasty and fattening. They cut your appetite and cheat you of the good food you really need." On and on he went, giving me all his theories about doughnuts—inflaming me with his hatred of doughnuts. But when he was through I wondered: why, if doughnuts are all bad, are millions of people buying them every day?

Cussing Communism has become a political and journalistic stock-in-trade in our country. Whether the "cussers" are irresponsible demagogues or sober, responsible national leaders, they usually leave unanswered the same question: why—if communism is all bad—why are millions of people buying it every day?

How can we account for this appeal of Communism? On the lowest level we may say that Communism appeals because of its emphatic concern with the *common needs of common men.* Underfed people are uncritical. They do not think "long, long thoughts" like Longfellow's youth, and their patience is as short as a baby's temper before feeding. They will believe and try anything that promises help soon, regardless of how untrustworthy the promise may appear to us from our well-fed point of view. To masses of hungry people Communism still seems to be the answer to the petition, "give us *this day* our daily bread," and it is obvious that men and women will continue to be deluded by this promise as long as they have to keep going to bed hungry night after night.

On a higher level, Communism appeals to the disinherited, outclassed people by its promise of *community* in places where there never has been anything but discrimination and oppression. Hunger creates a great sense of urgency in a man's stomach, the painful pressure of a void which must be filled in order to be relieved. But there is a hunger of the spirit which also clamors for satisfaction, though its ache is more patient and dull. It is the hunger for status, for a sense of personal worth, for self-respect bestowed upon us by our fellow-men simply because we too are human. Communism has been fearfully successful in passing itself off as the champion of human brotherhood, thanks to some measure of achievement magnified a thousandfold by all the known devices of propaganda. Such a claim may look preposterous to us, but not to millions of people who want to believe it because it raises in them the hope that the wistful emptiness of their souls may be filled on short order and by simple means.

On the highest level, the appeal of Communism is not and never has been wholly material or materialistic. It has been in the promise of a great cause to which *people may commit themselves.* Let us remember that Communism was not born in the mind of some ill-fed, ill-clad factory worker whose wife lay dying of consumption and whose children had hardly a gutter to call their own playground. Communism was born in the minds of men who had access to all the necessities of life as well as to most of its luxuries and who could have gone through life as virtuously self-satisfied as all of us are or tend to be. Nor did Communism win many recruits in this country among the people who, according to Communist vocabulary, might be called "proletarians." Rather, it captured the imagination of many men and women whose motivation was as idealistic and altruistic as their judgment was misguided and naive. For Communism is essentially a faith and a way of life, to be embraced with religious fervor and practiced with self-surrender; and to its adherents all the horrible, flagrant denials of its ideal in actual practice—the blood purges, the slave labor camps, the broken promises—can be and are being satisfactorily rationalized, not because they are all stupid but simply because their need for a cause, for an object of commitment, is at least as great as their need for bread. For we are fated to serve some Master, be it Mammon or God.

Nothing could be more trivial, nor more true, than to say that Communism is a menace. The question is: what is the nature of this menace and what can we do to conquer it? It seems to me that the most vocal foes of Communism among us are, on the one hand, overrating its danger and, on the other hand, underrating its challenge.

It is evident that Russian Communism today represents a *danger to our national security* as well as to the security of all nations that prefer freedom and responsible self-government to outside domination or home-bred puppet dictatorship. It is by no accident that a recent Social Education and Action Report of our General Assembly entitled its first so-called "area of concern," *Communism and National Defense.* Russian power represents a potential for military aggression which we could not possibly ignore unless we stretched the neck of the American eagle, put long feathers around his midriff, and stuck his head in the nearest pile of sand. On the other hand, the same report recommitted us as Presbyterians to "our historic opposition to Universal Military Training as a permanent peacetime program" because, while some fires may have to be fought with fire, no fire is ever extinguished by fire, nor is the threat of war ever averted by a military establishment so expensive that, in order to justify its existence, it has to welcome, and even seek, war.

Furthermore, no one will deny that there has been and undoubtedly still is a measure of *danger to our national security from within* and that every effort must be made by the proper agencies to uncover existing spies and saboteurs. Watchfulness is the price of security, but some of us have had severe misgivings about the propriety of certain investigations and the qualifications of certain investigators. Thinking in terms of our American legal and political heritage only, we wonder whether deep and far-reaching wrongs have not been done in the defense of the very things we know to be right, and whether the overprotection of our people and institutions from Communism may not make us so insecure and so emotionally dependent on our protectors that we may eventually welcome some form of American Fascism.

Thus the wholly *negative and hysterical approach to the Communist menace* is questionable even from the standpoint of social tradition, but it becomes completely untenable when we view it *in the light of our Christian faith.* To Christians, the assumption that everything is pitch black on the Communist side and that consequently everything must be snow-white on our side must appear not only as the height of arrogance but as the kind of attitude which can do and has already done much to estrange others both from our political and social ideals and from our Christianity, driving them straight into the arms, the welcoming arms of Communism. As critical as we are and must be, not only of the monstrous crimes committed in the name of Communism, but also of the patent flaws in the teachings of Communism, we dare not forget—and here we quote again the General Assembly's Report—we dare not forget that "many of the proclaimed goals of the Russian revolution are really distortions of valid Christian hopes and doctrines." As clearly as we must see the danger of Communism, we cannot ignore the fact that there are in Communist propaganda, and the very existence of Communism, some elements of valid criticism directed at our own imperfect practice of our ideals.

For one thing, Communism capitalizes on its recognition of man's legitimate *need for bread.* But Jesus, too, recognized this need, though not as the greatest need of man. He said, "Man shall not live by bread alone," but He did not say that man could or should expect to live without bread. If we think Communism is materialistic and Christianity spiritual, we must quickly redefine our terms. For the Christian faith centers around God's entrance in human *flesh.* The Christian symbols of divine forgiveness are the body and blood of our Lord, discerned in the equally material tokens of bread and wine; and according to Christ's own parable, our fate in the Judgment will depend on whether or not we have offered food to hungry mouths and drink to parched lips and stretched out a hand of mercy to the poor, the oppressed, and the sick. There is nothing abstractly "spiritual" in these essential facts of our faith. Instead there is a joyful recognition of our status as creatures of God with all the sins and vices of mortal flesh but with God's free forgiveness in Christ as our possession and prize, and with our God-given commission to transfigure our earthiness, not by pretending to be or to have disembodied spirits, nor by bemoaning the materialism of people who do not know how to be spiritual on an empty stomach, but by spending ourselves freely on behalf of our equally earthbound neighbors in Princeton, Germany, India, everywhere. The Voice of America may have potential for good, but we must not forget the voices of *Christian America,* not broadcast over the airwaves but wrapped up in unsolicited gift parcels of food and clothing; concealed in petitions demanding surplus wheat and surplus milk to be sent to starving people regardless of their politics; or translated into the kind of pledge to the church which represents not conventional condescending endorsement, but painfully sacrificial investment. These voices of Christian America are telling the world about a faith and way of life infinitely higher than Communism, higher even than Americanism, a faith and a way of life in which turning the other cheek is not just a Bible verse but a plan of action.

Communism also capitalizes on its promise of a society where social injustice and racial discrimination shall be forgotten, a society where the human *longing for community* will be fully expressed. Once again Communist propaganda is diabolically skillful in diverting the attention of its audience from the grotesquely dreadful flaws in Communism's record by self-righteously pointing at our less violent but equally sinful betrayals of our democratic ideals. By magnificent lies Communist propaganda may lead its audience to believe that the plight of our 15,000,000 American Negroes is comparable to the plight of the (let us say) 15,000,000 political prisoners perishing in Siberian slavery. The trouble is that there is *just enough truth* in the accusation to embarrass us profoundly and make us resolve as Christians not to rest until every remembrance of American ghettos—no matter who their victims are, no matter whether they be sanctioned by law or convention—forever disappears from our midst. Nor is there anything that can more completely refute such propaganda by removing its causes than the small but clear voice of the *worldwide Christian community,* deeply enmeshed in the sins of nations but increasingly humble and self-critical, penitent and courageous; a growing community within the nations whose ultimate end is to transcend and swallow up all national and racial differences in common allegiance to Christ, the Lord of all.

Finally, Communism capitalizes on its promise of a cause that demands complete *commitment.* To the Christian ear this strikes an old chord, but, let us face it, it is frequently a lost chord. Nothing is a more disheartening comment on our lack of vision and imagination than to talk wistfully about the good old days when Christians were thrown to the lions for their convictions because it was dangerous to be a Christian *then.* As if it were safe to be a Christian *now*, not only behind the Iron Curtain, mind you, but right here! Just pause sometimes long enough to ask yourself, "How long would I keep my job if I did and said all that my conscience, in the light of my faith, urges me to say and to do? How long would I be popular with my friends? How long would I spend my money the way I am doing now?" Let us not forget it. The most fertile breeding-ground for Communism and for its chameleonlike twin, Fascism, is not necessarily an underfed, disillusioned, jaded people, perishing not for lack of calories but for lack of a cause worth living for and dying for. America may be running a great risk in this direction unless we who are trying to be Christians allow our consciences to be so sensitized by that most disturbing Christ that our voice and actions in turn may launch our nation and government on new, uncharted seas of collective goodness and righteousness, through a fresh commitment to Him Who is Lord not only over the church but over America and over the whole world.

What shall be our answer to the appeal, menace, and challenge of Communism? The Social Education and Action report of our General Assembly puts is into strong, straightforward words:

> Let us make our Christian ideals, of which the goals of the Russian revolution are heresies, really work in our part of the world. A vital application of these teachings in words and deeds would be the most telling demonstration of Christian truth and the best answer to Communist claims.

What else did Paul mean when he wrote: "Bless those who persecute you; bless and do not curse them. . . . If possible, so far as it depends upon you, live peaceably with all. . . . Do not be overcome by evil but overcome evil with good.

Comment: The Church Faces Communism

The sermon cleared the air by bringing the subject into the open in the congregation and the community. While preaching, I spotted in the balcony the bulky form of one of the Trustees, a local merchant who had not set foot in the church since I signed on. He was taking copious notes. Whatever use he made or intended to make of them, he could have saved himself the trouble: copies of the sermon were available in the narthex at the close of the service.

Far more important, I saw that Dr. John A. Mackay, President of Princeton Seminary, was in his accustomed pew with brittle, quick-witted Mrs. Mackay. Just a month later, Dr. Mackay would publish his *Letter to Presbyterians,* which would drive the first, large nail into Senator McCarthy's political coffin. It is possible that the sermon played some modest part in the formation of Dr. Mackay's *Letter.* Nothing would please or flatter me more than to find out that it did!

One might think, after the dissolution of the Soviet Union and its "evil empire," that this sermon should be filed and forgotten. Perhaps. But, on second thought, Communism is hardly dead: over one billion people still live under its rule. Nor is McCarthyism dead, except by that name. The single-issue politics and murderous ruthlessness of the Pro-Life Movement, the recently exposed potential for large-scale violence by the so-called militias, the newly virulent discrimination against immigrants, both legal and illegal, are symptoms of a drift toward a revival of McCarthyism—by whatever name. "Left" or "Right" have long been misnomers. The real enemy of democracy, of civil liberties, of civil rights is totalitarianism, whether of the Left or of the Right. Historically dated, the sermon may yet prove disquietingly relevant.

THE RIGHT TO BE A WANTED CHILD

Context: The Right To Be a Wanted Child

I preached this sermon in Princeton at the First (now Nassau) Presbyterian Church on October 9, 1955, in my fourth year as pastor of the church. During the previous year we had been able to dedicate some significant additions to our church plant. The church was growing, but it was still just the second largest church in Princeton. St. Paul's Roman Catholic Church was by far the largest.

St. Paul's was located only a few blocks from the center of Princeton, but the psychic and social distance was far greater. There was no formal contact between St. Paul's and any of the other Christian churches, which St. Paul's would not have recognized as fully Christian. The Second Vatican Council was less than a decade away but in 1955 it could not even be imagined.

The crisis broke out so suddenly that I did not have time even to advise Session of my decision to address it in a sermon. I felt confident, however, that the congregation would agree with, or at least respect, my position. I do not recall whether or not the Presbyterian Church, USA was already on record in favor of family planning.

This is what was happening. The Community Chest had just admitted to membership the Princeton Chapter of the Planned Parenthood League (PPL). The priest of St. Paul's Church was incensed. He ordered his parishioners to boycott the Chest's annual fund drive, which was about to start, unless PPL withdrew from membership. The timetable of events was such that I had to take the issue into the pulpit the very next Sunday—or miss the boat.

Writing this sermon was a struggle not just because of the pressure of time but for two substantive reasons. For one thing, the only explicit statement on the subject I could find in the Bible was God's command, in Genesis 1:28. "Be fruitful and multiply, and fill the earth and subdue it. . . ." Dating from a time of acute UNDERpopulation, the commandment becomes a prescription for collective suicide in an age of worsening OVERpopulation. Paul Ehrlich's blockbuster, *The Population Bomb*, would dramatically confirm this reading of the situation—years later. Meanwhile, I was having to argue from the spirit of the Bible against the letter of the Bible!

I also realized that the argument from numbers might be indicted as callous, elitist, cynical. It would not do for me to belabor the well-known statistics showing how many million babies were being born each year, not just in India or China but in our own country, to people who could not afford them. Instead I decided to take the baby's part, to dramatize the hardship and heartbreak that awaits every unwanted child, to affirm the need for a social policy that will guarantee every child's right to be a wanted child.

THE RIGHT TO BE A WANTED CHILD

By John R. Bodo
Pastor
First (now Nassau) Presbyterian Church
Princeton, New Jersey
October 9, 1955

SCRIPTURE: GENESIS 1:29–31
MATTHEW 18:1–6

Nursery rhymes are so well fixed in the curly heads of our children that we dare not change as much as one word in any of them. But if we dare not tamper with the familiar words, we may at least add another verse now and then. Take this classic for instance:

> There was an old woman who lived in a shoe,
> She had so many children, she didn't know what to do,
> She fed them on milk without any bread,
> Then spanked them all soundly, and put them to bed.

Now add to this something to bring the moral up to date:

> She let them grow wild like tumbleweed
> To law and order they paid little heed,
> For haphazard children are a contingency
> Which often ends in juvenile delinquency.

The serious meaning behind this modest attempt at humor is only too clear. It came home to me more forcefully than ever in a statement quoted in Benjamin Fine's startling *One Million Delinquents*: "Behind today's headlines of crime and juvenile delinquency stands a small, sorrowful figure—yesterday's unhappy child who somehow failed to take root in a secure home."

I. PLANNED PARENTHOOD—A PROTESTANT VIEW

As Americans, we take pride in our conviction that everyone has certain native rights: the right to life, to liberty, and to the pursuit of happiness. But these rights do not wait for our arrival in the world. The granting or denial of these rights depends, to an extraordinary degree, upon the admission of a more basic right: the right to be wanted by one's parents—the right to be a wanted child.

I do not propose to preach planned parenthood on the level of its practicality or social desirability alone. The preaching on these levels is being done by a competent organization which an increasing number of Americans admire and support. What I hope to do is to set the ideal of planned parenthood in a Christian perspective. This is important not only because the Catholic Church is committed to an attitude of militant antagonism to planned parenthood, but primarily because the aims of planned parenthood are consistent with the social teachings of the major Protestant churches, which in turn are derived from the Bible.

In turning to the Bible, however, we must bear in mind that we cannot expect to find there any specific instructions, pro or con, concerning medical discoveries and scientific techniques which were not known to man until almost two thousand years later. Any attempt to prove from the Bible that a certain method of birth control or child spacing is right or wrong should be condemned as historically impossible and intellectually unsound.

On the other hand, there is much in the Bible to indicate that God does not consider human multiplication as the be-all and end-all of creation. If we chose to be quite literalistic for a moment, we might note that God ordered Adam and Eve to "be fruitful and multiply" when it was quite safe to do so because there were just the two of them in the whole world! The same divine injunction was given to Noah and his family—after the Flood. Speaking more seriously, we may recall that in the Creation story God fills the earth with all the things necessary to meet man's needs, so that man may feel welcome and secure immediately upon his creation. We may also remember that the social problems caused by overpopulation were not unfamiliar even in Old Testament times, and that in many instances the prophets interpreted the distress of their overpopulated nation or territory as a judgment of God.

But in all the Bible, nothing seems to support the case for planned parenthood more conclusively than Christ's own attitude toward children. I cannot help feeling that the Master whose love of children was so intense would be more deeply distressed by what we call juvenile delinquency than by any other symptom of our moral and social deterioration. I cannot help feeling that He who set a little child in the midst of His disciples to explain to them the meaning of God's kingdom, would not hesitate to pick up the whip again and use it on those who, sometimes in His very name, encourage ignorance and irresponsibility which populate the world with unwanted children.

II. PLANNED PARENTHOOD—THE CATHOLIC VIEW

Now let me say at once that the Catholic Church is not opposed to all birth control. As a matter of fact, the Papal Encyclical on *Christian Marriage,* issued by Pius XI in 1930, endorses two methods and at least condones a third. The first method permitted to Catholics is celibacy. From the point of view of the population problem, this method is impractical to say the least. People ought to be free to stay single, whether for religious or any other reasons, but to expect a sufficient number of people to stay celibate for the sake of the nation's or the world's social health is rather utopian.

The second method permitted to Catholics is continence. Apart from any abstract merit or demerit, the practical value of this method is even more doubtful. To quote a phrase from Joseph Fletcher's provocative book, *Morals and Medicine*: "Even St. Paul, whose teachings on sex and marriage were very strict, never suggests that the creation of offspring is the only justification for sexual intercourse between husband and wife. On the contrary, it is he who reminds us of God's design by which a man and a woman in marriage become "one flesh" not for any ulterior motive but for the sake of that mysterious union which is in itself a worthy symbol of Christ's union with His Church.

Ruling out celibacy and continence, then, as methods of control unlikely to make more than a dent in the problem of unwanted children, we are left with the third method permitted to Catholics and with the real issue around which the battle is being waged.

This method, condoned by Pope Pius XI, fervently welcomed by Catholic theologians in their forced retreat from their previous total opposition, and known as the "rhythm" method, is somewhat too technical to be expounded here, as well as too familiar to need such expounding. We may say just a word or two. For one thing, the moral distinction between "hoping to be safe" and "being safe," is fuzzy and hypocritical. If God wills an unlimited number of children, then any interference with His will is a sin, whether such interference be more passive or more active. On the other hand, there is no reason to believe that God wills anything of the sort, or that the Catholic method for planned parenthood is more "Christian" than any other humane, rational, and socially acceptable method.

If the issue were really interference with God's will by getting in the way of something He intends to accomplish through the processes of nature, then, quoting Paul Blanshard, we should also "oppose shaving, the removal of tonsils, and the straightening of teeth." For that matter, Blanshard goes on, "celibacy itself is far more 'against nature' than contraception because it means the thwarting of one of man's most powerful instincts for the whole adolescent and adult life of the individual." But then, Blanshard concludes, "reason and logic now play a decidedly secondary role in the Catholic war against birth control. The Pope has spoken, and the doctrine against contraception must be defended as divine and eternal." (*American Freedom and Catholic Power,* Beacon Press, 1950, p. 144)

III. THE CONSEQUENCES OF UNPLANNED PARENTHOOD

But we need not dwell any longer on the inconsistency of the Catholic position. The last thing we want is to be *for* something because somebody else is *against* it. Let us rather take a brief look at the consequences of unplanned parenthood.

A minister gets so much literature promoting worthy causes that he develops a regrettable immunity to them. Nevertheless, I defy even the most hardened minister to read this statistical item without taking it upon his conscience and into his pulpit.

"About 4,000,000 babies were born in the U.S. in 1953, according to the National Office of Vital Statistics. About 1,000,000 criminal abortions were performed in the U.S. during the same period, according to conservative estimates. Some informed people think that the annual abortion total may actually run as high as 1,500,000." This item appears in a pamphlet published by the Planned Parenthood Federation of America and is entitled *Breaking the Vicious Circle.*

But for every child who is killed before birth for want of planning, there are many more who are permitted to live, much to their own misfortune. Nor do they all live in old shoes or shacks. Some of them live in penthouses. The tragedy is the same: they are unwanted. According to some scientists like Karl Menninger, children may have emotional experiences even before birth. If that is the case, then the mother's anxiety, frustration, and resentment of her unborn child will surely be communicated. And if such a grave handicap may be felt even by the unborn child, it is no wonder that he will grow up unhappy, rebellious, and antisocial in behavior—another victim of the vicious circle!

The final consequence of unplanned parenthood may seem remote to the nearsighted, but it is actually the major force behind the present unrest of three-fourths of the human race. The welcome disintegration of colonialism and white supremacy is but a symptom of this force. The rise and diabolical growth of Communism is but another symptom. The driving force behind all these cataclysmic symptoms is none other than the sudden and frightening growth of the world's population. If you like "shockers," do not waste your time on "kid stuff" like *Dracula* or *The Thing.* Read *Human Breeding and Survival* by Burch and Pendell. For thirty-five cents, these two cool-headed, fact-minded sociologists will treat you to a vision of "war, famine, and pestilence" which dwarfs in both scope and horror the visions of St. John of Patmos. The only difference is that this vision is a scientific prognostic based on the assumption of continued resistance to planned parenthood, and on the resulting overpopulation of the earth.

It is the duty and privilege of all churches to guide men and women in the founding and maintaining of Christian homes. The first Community Church of Columbus, Ohio, has long been a leader in this most modern, and at the same time, most evangelical, ministry to families. It is from the pastor of this great church, Dr. Roy A. Burkhart, that I want to borrow my conclusion.

"Man," Dr. Burkhart writes, "is the only living creature with rational control over his own reproduction. In the evolution of man we find a movement toward a qualitative rather than a quantitative goal. It is not how many years a man lives that is important, it is how much, how fully he lives. It is not how many children he has: it is the quality of their characters, the quality of their spirits that is most important . . . And where can men use the power of reason and apply the capacity of planning to more good than in bringing their children into the world in such a way that they are not only wanted, but that they come at such intervals and in such numbers as to grow up with the greatest capacity to share . . . with the creative God in creative living." (Roy A. Burkhart, *Ministerial Counselling and Planned Parenthood,* PPFA, 501 Madison Avenue, New York 22, New York. p. 20)

These are the words of an outstanding spiritual leader, but their authority is no more than the sense they make or, rather, than the faithfulness with which they reflect the spirit of Another——the spirit of Him who on a quite ordinary day put his arms around a little child and said: "Whoever receives one such child in my name receives me; but whoever causes one of these little ones to stumble, it would be better for him to have a great millstone fastened around his neck and be drowned in the depth of the sea." (Matthew 18:5–6)

Comment: The Right to Be a Wanted Child

The sermon was enthusiastically received. I wondered, though, whether by highlighting one of the serious disagreements between Protestants and Catholics, or at least the Roman hierarchy, I might have inadvertently fanned the flames of anti-Catholic bigotry which had defeated Al Smith in 1928 and would nearly defeat John F. Kennedy in 1960.

The Planned Parenthood League did withdraw from membership in the Community Chest. The priest's blackmail scored, to that extent. But a month later PPL's independent fund drive yielded triple of the previous year's allocation to PPL from the Community Chest. And what PPL gained in public recognition and respect exceeded any material benefits.

On the basis of numerous comments at the time, I have reason to believe that the sermon accounted for a respectable percentage of both the material and the spiritual components of PPL's victory—that it struck a blow for the principle of responsible family planning. Of course I cannot prove this. But I am pleased to recall that "The Right To Be a Wanted Child" was published as a pamphlet by the national PPL the same year, and that it enjoyed wide distribution, at least through the Fifties.

WHO IS MY NEIGHBOR?

Context: Who Is My Neighbor?

I preached this sermon at First (now Nassau) Presbyterian Church, Princeton, on May 19, 1957. It marked my most public involvement in a social justice issue during my Princeton pastorate (1951–1959). It is probably the most important sermon I ever preached.

Princeton's Negro residents had long been cooped up along Witherspoon Street, which starts right at historic Nassau Hall. The area allotted to them was about twelve blocks long and just two blocks wide. By 1957, many Negro families could afford to buy or rent better housing, but the ghetto walls held.

First Church, standing on the university campus just a couple of hundred feet from Nassau Hall, began as a racially integrated congregation—after a fashion. Negroes were members, though separate rolls of "White Communicants" and "Black Communicants" were kept, and they were seated in the balcony only. But when the church was rebuilt, after the fire of 1836, the balcony was not replaced: the Negroes allegedly preferred to organize their own worship, in the ghetto.

Thus was born, in 1837, the Witherspoon Street Presbyterian Church. Paul Robeson would grow up in that church, under his father's pastoral leadership. And in the 1950s, there was the Rev. Benjamin J. Anderson, another marvelous bass, and a prime mover in the struggle for civil rights and specifically for open housing. Thanks to his friendship and example, I joined the struggle.

Concurrently, the Presbyterian Church, USA was coming to life about the issue of racial discrimination and a segregated housing market. The 1956 General Assembly adopted a statement in favor of open housing, urging congregations to enter into "covenants of open occupancy"—as a counterweight to the prevailing system of racially restrictive covenants. Session's Committee on Social Education and Action embraced the idea and persuaded Session to endorse the covenant and to submit it to the congregation.

The mailing would include: a cover letter from Session; a reprint of the General Assembly's action proposing covenants of open occupancy; the covenant itself, designed for individual signatures, so that a husband might sign while his wife might not, or vice versa; and a notice about the newly organized, interfaith Princeton Housing Group, a vehicle for citizen action. The four-page mailing (reprinted after the sermon) went out on a Saturday, deliberately, so that I might preach on the subject on Sunday.

The time was ripe. The issue had been joined for months between the Princeton Housing Authority and residents of the ghetto. Most recently, the Mayor's Advisory Committee on Housing had reported to the Borough Council that there was no solution to the housing problem in the ghetto, except to allow and assist economically qualified Negro families to gain access to housing outside the ghetto. But nothing was happening, so the time was ripe.

The biblical basis of the sermon is the concept of *neighbor*, with Luke 10:25–29 and Romans 13:8–10 illustrating the concern rather than determining its direction. Essential to the treatment is the understanding that, in the Bible, neighbor really means neighbor rather than "fellow-human," so that, as Christians, we are commanded to let people close to us and learn to live with them, help them, love them at close range, no matter how different from us they may be or seem to be.

Another essential aspect of the treatment is the unmasking of the hypocrisy which underlies the system of residential segregation. Negroes had been living all over Princeton for 200 years—as maids, cooks, butlers, gardeners, caretakers. They had been and continued to be intimately involved with their white "masters" and their families. No problem, as long as they knew—and kept—their "place"!

WHO IS MY NEIGHBOR?

By John R. Bodo
Pastor
First (now Nassau) Presbyterian Church
Princeton, New Jersey
May 19, 1957

SCRIPTURE: LUKE 10:25–29
ROMAN 13:8–10

Tomorrow or the next day you will receive from the Session a little document giving you an opportunity as members of this church and citizens of this community to go on record, individually, in favor of equal opportunity in housing. It is no secret that every tenth Princeton resident is forced to live in a strictly defined area, just because of his complexion. The Session, following the action of the 1956 General Assembly of the Presbyterian Church, has studied the problem from the standpoint of both civic and Christian concern and is now laying it upon your conscience.

To be sure, segregation is not peculiar to Princeton. It is still the prevailing pattern, South and North. In the North great progress has been made in many phases of the problem, especially since World War II. Princeton has shared in this progress by gradually equalizing opportunities in education, in public accommodations, in employment. But the housing barrier—patterned on the ghetto system of the Middle Ages—stands fast.

Against this local background, it may be worthwhile to explore some of the reasons why the ancient question, "Who is my neighbor?" should receive our renewed attention, and why the implied question, "Who may be my neighbor?" should be raised in the oldest church of Princeton.

I. THE BIBLE ON NEIGHBORS

What guidance do we find in the Bible on this problem? All of our life we have been hearing and repeating the Ten Commandments and their summary enthroned by Jesus as the supreme commandment, "Thou shalt love the Lord Thy God . . . and thy neighbor as thyself." If we were asked who is meant by the word "neighbor," we would probably answer that in the Christian perspective all our fellow-men are our neighbors, especially in this shrunken world of ours. But the biblical meaning of neighbor was primarily geographic. In the context of Palestinian society, "neighbor" meant the man next door or a few doors up or down, because villages were very small and common defense and other interest demanded physical nearness. There were other laws for the conduct of the Jews toward strangers and foreigners, but the law of neighborly love was God's law for a neighborhood—literally.

For a good neighbor was a great asset. In Proverbs 27:10 we are reminded, "Better a neighbor that is near than a brother that is far off," which is like saying, "a friend in need is a friend indeed"—if he is near enough when I need him! On the other hand, the temptations of neighborhood are realistically admitted in the Old Testament. What could be more candid as well as contemporary than "Thou shalt not covet thy neighbor's house, thou shalt not covet thy neighbor's wife, nor his power mower, nor his station wagon, nor anything that is thy neighbor's?" We dare not push away from us the homely edge of God's law. The Bible shows that the awareness of human brotherhood under a common heavenly Father was born, nurtured, and refined in neighborhood situations, complete with front lawns, back fences, and children playing together.

It is on this foundation that Christ's Law of Love is built. The story of the Good Samaritan assumes all the rich meaning of the word "neighbor" and then enlarges it to include others to whose presence we might not be accustomed, and whom, in our ignorance, we might fear or scorn. For the real point of the story is not that we should help our fellow-men when they are down, but that a fellow-man whom we may have been excluding from our fellowship—from our "neighborhood"—might prove to be a more genuine neighbor than even some of the most distinguished members of our own in-group, club, or race—whatever that word means.

II. THE EFFECTS OF THE GHETTO ON NEGROES

Now residential segregation in Princeton has received considerable official and public recognition in recent months. It would not be proper for me to comment—at this time and in this place—on the efforts of the Borough Housing Authority and the subsequent discussion between the Borough Council and a citizens' committee from the affected area. It is my understanding, however, that the Mayor's Advisory Committee on Housing, in its latest report, makes it unequivocally clear that there can be no permanent solution to the problem of the Witherspoon-John Street area until all parts of our community become open to all persons, subject only to such economic limitations as apply to all of us.

But Christian concern with any public issue is always personal rather than technical. Technical considerations are important and cannot be lightly dismissed in the name of abstract principle, but for the citizen who strives to think and act primarily as a Christian, the main question must always be, "What is the human side of this issue? What is happening to people as a result of this state of things?"

It is on this personal level that the deepest psychological and spiritual damage is being inflicted on Negro Princetonians. No one can fully develop his God-given potential as a person unless he is free—as free as the next person—to take a responsible part in the life of his community according to his individual ability and inclination. The issue is not integration *per se*. The issue is freedom. As long as we actively perpetuate or passively condone a system which makes it impossible for an otherwise fully qualified Negro family to live on our street, we are accessories to robbery. We are robbing our fellow-citizens and fellow-Christians of their freedom just as effectively as if those "ghetto" walls were real walls, with the doors left open during certain hours and under certain conditions, but in this respect, tightly shut and bolted on our side.

Oh, it would do some of us a great deal of good to change places–if only for one week—with a Negro Princetonian in search of a house or building lot! Our purpose would not be to prove an abstract point. It would be as simple as finding a better place to live, with a spacious yard for the children and an environment more adequately reflecting our economic, cultural, and social level. What an eye-opener it would be for us, in our dark disguise, to make the rounds and get the "run-around"—to be told by agents that they have nothing to suit our needs when the newspapers scream with their "for sale" ads, to hit snag after snag in conversations with well-meaning but uninformed, conventional people! With what shame and indignation would we come back to resume our fair skin and to take our stand with the forces that will not rest until Princeton becomes at last one community, "indivisible, with liberty and justice for all!"

III. THE EFFECTS OF THE GHETTO ON US

For if the effects of residential segregation on Negro Princetonians are damaging as well as obvious, the effects upon us are equally damaging though more subtle.

For one thing, segregation keeps us in a state of uneasiness and apprehension. The day of "white supremacy" is done throughout the world. The non-white majority of mankind has caught up with our technological advantage, or is catching up fast. Millions of hands—yellow, brown, and black—are reaching for the abundant life. Through our foreign aid program we endeavor to grasp these hands in friendship and to work out a partnership in the defense of freedom and peace. But our hands are sticky—sticky with nearly a hundred years of unfulfilled promises—and the Russians, whose hands are sticky with the blood of millions, still manage to pose as the friends and saviors of the colored peoples of the world by making sure that they know all about Emmett Till and Autherine Lucy and the so-called "code of ethics" of America's real estate brokers.

So we fear the march of history in a vague, haunting way, but—paradoxically—we fear our friends even more. The unforgivable sin in our day seems to be nonconformity. A pamphlet published by the American Friends Service Committee has the significant title *They Say That You Say*. Its thesis is that continued residential segregation cannot be blamed on the real estate brokers or anyone else—except on ourselves. We worry about what our friends might say if we stepped out of line, and they worry about what we might say if they stepped out of line, until we are all trapped in a strange ghetto of our own—a spiritual ghetto—whose walls are made of unexamined assumptions, and within whose bounds we live like carbon copies of one another, outdoing one another in that most un-American trait—conformity.

But the spot where residential segregation hurts us the most is our conscience. As Americans in general and Princetonians in particular, we are committed to the ideals of John Witherspoon, Woodrow Wilson, and many others like them. But this heritage of Christian and democratic ideals weighs on our hearts with an aching weight. The more we cherish our past, the more painful the present becomes with its big words and small deeds. Negro Americans and Negro Princetonians are the only ones whose conscience need not and does not hurt at this crucial point. They did not ask to come here in the first place: our ancestors brought their ancestors over by force. They did not ask to be cheated of the fruits of their freedom, once freedom became the law of the land: our great-grandfathers, South and North, made sure that their freedoms would remain largely on the books. Even now, nearly a century after the Emancipation Proclamation, they are asking only that we begin at last to keep our own laws—that we become what we say we are; and they are pleading their case with all the dignity and power of a clear conscience, while all of us—whether we are *pro* or *con*—must live with a corroding sense of guilt, for no other reason than that we are free, white, and over twenty-one!

IV. THE CHRISTIAN POTENTIAL

Now what is the Christian potential of equal opportunity in housing? What would happen, specifically from the Christian point of view, if through your witness and friendly endeavors Princeton should become what you have long desired it to be—an effective, unself-conscious showcase of American democracy at its best?

For one thing, the opening of all Princeton to all residents on the basis of individual merit alone would strike at the roots of one of our gravest sins as Christians—the sin of pride. I do not mean being proud of worthwhile accomplishments and cherished possessions. I mean pride in the biblical sense—the arrogant, unwarranted exalting of ourselves at the expense of others. Just remember one ironic fact: Princeton is a residentially integrated community right now, because Negroes can and do live everywhere—right in our homes—as servants. They may live under the same roof with us, minister to our most basic needs, share our life at the closest range—as long as they do not forget their "place," their inferior status which our infantile craving for superiority demands. If this be not sin, what is sin?

Again, the opening of all Princeton to all residents on the basis of individual merit alone, would help our churches become what God designed them to be and what they actually claim to be. For if there is one fellowship in a community where persons should be together regardless of all incidental differences, the churches should be that fellowship. Unfortunately this is usually not the case. At a conference I attended a few weeks ago, D. T. Niles of Ceylon reminded us that "fellowship" in the New Testament is always a noun, because it is conceived as God's gift through Jesus Christ, in Whom we have a unity more fundamental than any of our divisions. But, he went on to say, in this country we have made "fellowship" into a verb, to indicate how little we care for our God-given unity in Christ and how much we prefer to associate with one another on the basis of superficial likeness, until our churches become little more than mutual admiration societies.

The shoe fits. We dare not deny that the churches of Princeton—and this church in particular—have not been in the vanguard. As Christians we can ill afford to point our fingers, for the finger we point always turns around to point at us. Right here, in the sanctuary, we are still—not by law, not by direct intention, but in lame statistical fact—a segregated church. And my conviction is that our broken fellowship will never be restored at all unless you, as Christian citizens, help to take down the wall which is the main cause of our continued division as Christians—the wall of the ghetto by which our impulse to Christian togetherness has been effectively contained and well-nigh stifled.

May I close with a little personal confession, quite typical and quite damning: I have not always said or even known the things I have said today. Or rather, I knew them in theory but did not feel them in my flesh and bones. I got through five years in a church in Newark without ever discovering the problem, because the nearest Negro lived a mile away and might as well have lived on another continent. But even in this church—half a block from Witherspoon Street and three blocks from our sister church—I got through two years without really facing the problem, so high and strong are the walls of the ghetto. Even to the most "broadminded" among us, something special must happen to awaken him and to help him discover his brothers on the other side of the wall.

How did it happen to me? I wish I knew. I am reminded of a science fiction story in which there was a whole fascinating world enveloping New York in another dimension, impinging on the city at all points but unknown to New Yorkers except when one of them inadvertently fell through the hole. I forget where the hole was supposed to be or what it was supposed to symbolize in the story. But, speaking of my pilgrimage through Princeton, I humbly thank God for that unremembered day when He caused me to fall through the hole. For in my discovery of that other Princeton—among the missing ten percent—my experience of the potential glory of America and the fullness of the Church of Jesus Christ has been deepened and enlarged far beyond my deserving.

So tomorrow or the next day when you receive your "covenant of open occupancy" from our Session, remember: it may be your road map to the hole—to the hole in your private ghetto wall—through which God may guide you into a fresh dimension of love and fellowship and into a more faithful obedience to His commandment, "Thou shalt love—thy neighbor—as thyself."

NOTE: This sermon was subsequently published in *The Pulpit Speaks on Race*, edited by Alfred T. Davies (New York: Abingdon Press, 1965), pp. 119–26.

I am attaching a copy of the May 20, 1957, mailing from the Session to the congregation of First (Nassau) Presbyterian Church of Princeton.

The Session

First Presbyterian Church
Princeton, New Jersey
May 20, 1957

TOWARD EQUAL OPPORTUNITY IN HOUSING

Dear Fellow Church Members:

At the April 15 meeting of the Session of our Church, the attached *Covenant of Open Occupancy*—as drafted by the Department of Social Education and Action of the Presbyterian Church, U.S.A.—was unanimously adopted. You will note that this covenant is an outgrowth of the "Pronouncement on Residential Segregation" of the 168th General Assembly, a copy of which is also attached.

Both the Session and its Committee on Social Concern felt that all members of our church should be given an opportunity personally to commit themselves to this covenant. To this end, the Session requests all *adult* members—whose conscience so inclines them—to sign the attached *Covenant of Open Occupancy* and to return it to me in the enclosed self-addressed envelope before June 15.

Attached you will also find a brief description of the *Princeton Housing Group*, a local citizens group interested in the furtherance of equal opportunity in housing in Princeton. Would you care to know more about the work of this group? Would you be willing to have the group contact you if they feel that you may be of help in specific cases? Please indicate your response to these two questions on your signed covenant.

Cordially yours,
GEORGE M. GRACE
Housing Chairman
Committee on Social Concern

THE COMMITTEE ON SOCIAL CONCERN

John R. Arscott (Chairman)
Mrs. Stephen K. Bailey
Henry S. Broad
Charles M. Burrill
Mrs. Lefferts A. Loetscher
J. Donald Butler
Mrs. Robert R. Cawley
William S. Dix
George M. Grace
Lester L. Tibbals, Jr.

PRONOUNCEMENT OF THE 168TH GENERAL ASSEMBLY OF THE PRESBYTERIAN CHURCH, U.S.A. MAY 30, 1956 ON RESIDENTIAL SEGREGATION

"Emphasizing that it is the policy and purpose of the Presbyterian Church in the U.S.A. to work for a non-segregated society as well as a non-segregated church:

noting (1) that in many sections of our country real progress has been made in eliminating segregation in such fields as employment, transportation, hotel and restaurant accommodations, education, and other public services.

(2) that in these same sections where residential desegregation has occurred, it has always been in older housing areas that tend to change from segregated white to segregated non-white because of the flight of the white residents; and

(3) that in most communities practically no new homes have been made available to non-white families.

The 168th General Assembly

Calls upon Christians who are contemplating the sale of property to see as of first importance the need of minority families for equal housing opportunities and adequate housing, and to make their houses available to all qualified purchasers without regard to race;

Directs the attention of home-owners to several studies, available from the Department of Social Education and Action, of the effect on non-white purchases on adjacent property values, demonstrating that values do not necessarily decline, and in fact often rise, after such purchases;

Urges Session to bring Christians together in *covenants of open occupancy* which will stem the tendency toward 'panic selling' and stabilize their neighborhoods on a nonsegregated basis."

THE PRINCETON HOUSING GROUP
May 1957

In the greater Princeton area, as in so many other sections of the United States, it is very difficult for Negroes or members of other minority groups to buy houses or rent any accommodations, except in certain well-defined neighborhoods.

The Princeton Housing Group is working at this in various ways:

(1) By getting interested buyers and sellers together;

(2) By working on any problems of neighborhood or social adjustment which may arise;

(3) By holding occasional public meetings for education in this field;

(4) By being ready to cooperate with any organizations desiring help or information.

The desire of the Princeton Housing Group is not for integration *per se*, but for freedom:

Freedom for everyone to be treated on his own merits as an individual;

Freedom for everyone to enter the housing market for the satisfaction of his own needs and tastes, subject only to such economic and other considerations which apply to all.

Officers of the Princeton Housing Group

Mrs. L. V. Chandler, Convener
Mrs. Sherman Bates
Werner M. Blumenthal
Leonard F. Newton
Mrs. David R. Saunders
David S. Thompson

NOTE: Please sign and return in the enclosed envelope by June 15, 1957.

COVENANT OF OPEN OCCUPANCY

Acknowledging the call of the 168th General Assembly to all Presbyterians to form "covenants of open occupancy" which will promote inclusive residential patterns, mitigate "panic selling," and stabilize our neighborhood on a non-segregated basis,

THE UNDERSIGNED DO HEREBY ADOPT THIS COVENANT

(1) To support one another, and all others who refuse to conform to racial discrimination in housing, with friendship, mutual aid, and corporate action to prevent either social ostracism or economic reprisal because of our practice of nondiscrimination.

(2) To make known to our neighbors, if there is a tendency toward panic selling, that we will not sell our houses to escape racial integration but will urge others to stay and help maintain the standards of our community and all institutions and agencies.

(3) To make known to our neighbors whose houses are for sale or rent that we would welcome into the neighborhood any new residents of good character regardless of their race, creed, or national origin.

(4) To discuss thoughtfully and sensitively with our neighbors, when circumstances are appropriate, the meaning of open-occupancy housing and this Covenant, giving assurance that we, its signers, are deeply concerned about the permanent welfare of this community, and that if we move for other reasons, we will sell or rent our homes only to qualified purchasers or tenants of good character, without regard to their race, creed, or national origin.

(5) To seek to enlist our neighbors, whether or not they are members of the Presbyterian Church, to commit themselves to these same principles of action.

SIGNED

(Adult Church Members)

1.__________________________ 3.__________________________

2.__________________________ 4.__________________________

I would like to know more about the work of the Princeton Housing Group.

Yes No (Circle one)

I would be willing to have the Princeton Housing Group contact me if I might be of help in specific situations.

Yes No (Circle one)

Comment: Who Is My Neighbor?

What effect did "Who Is My Neighbor?" and the Covenant of Open Occupancy have on Princeton? About one-third of the households in First Church contributed at least one signature in favor of an open housing market. About half of the signers expressed an interest in the Princeton Housing Group (PHG). As a result, PHG was able to begin operating as an amateur real estate agency, helping black people find willing sellers and then holding hands with worried white neighbors, so that there would be no panic, no flight.

Within a year, PHG also went into business as Princeton Housing Associates, with George Otto and Morris Milgram, pioneer builders of interracial housing in the Philadelphia area and eventually all over the Northeast and Midwest. The two developments they helped us create in Princeton—Glen Acres, 18 homes, and Maplecrest, 25 homes—sold out according to the desired "balanced formula" (60 percent white) and survive to this day as showcases of successful residential integration. It may be appropriate to keep in mind that in 1957-58 there were no fair housing laws in the United States, at any level.

What effect did the action have on the First Church congregation? The issue was explosive. During the weeks following the sermon, I worked overtime listening to alarmed, indignant or just plain worried members, nearly all of them starting with "Now you know I am not prejudiced, but . . ." and similar bromides. When the dust settled, however, we discovered that no more than a dozen active members were withdrawing from the church because of "Who Is My Neighbor?" Twice as many members went to work in the Princeton Housing Group or lent a hand in connection with individual sales to Blacks. Nor was there any literal explosion, any violence, beyond someone's cutting the clothesline of a new black neighbor!

The procedure we used turned out to be a working model of effective social action through the local church. The action was corporate (General Assembly and Session) but properly individualized (Covenant) so that no one could claim to be misrepresented: if you did not sign, you were not involved. Most important, channeling a congregational initiative at once into a community organization (PHG) gave the effort on behalf of an open housing market the wide base it needed.

For my part, helping to organize an interfaith Princeton Pastors' Association, being cofounder—with Ben Anderson—of the Princeton Housing Group, and launching the initial campaign for fair housing in Princeton, remain among the most satisfying experiences of my fifty years in the Presbyterian ministry. A number of friendships formed around "Who Is My Neighbor?" endure to this day.

RIOT AT EPHESUS

Context: Riot at Ephesus

In the decade following World War II, there was a slight surge of interest in relating Christian faith to daily work. The Ecumenical Institute of the World Council of Churches convened conferences of Christians, men and women in various occupations, challenging them, through Bible study and theological reflection, to explore what specific difference Christian faith might or should make in the workaday life of a high school teacher, a factory foreman, a bricklayer, a fashion model, or a homemaker. The Department of the Church and Economic Life of the National Council of Churches also published a number of stimulating pamphlets on the subject, which had been almost totally neglected in post-Reformation Protestantism. First Church, Princeton, a congregation of mostly professional people, should be open to such exploration and should be able to marshal the requisite leadership talent.

I broached the idea to Session's Social Concerns Committee. No one could recall a single instance in which the subject had been dealt with in the church, whether in a sermon or in an adult course. Nor could we think of more than just a few biblical texts that seemed to relate to the faith-work nexus. For my part, I already had Acts 19:23–41 up my sleeve!

I hoped to relate the sermon to Labor Day, but the Sunday of Labor Day weekend is known to have the second lowest attendance (after the Sunday after Easter) in the whole year. Nor was it possible to follow the sermon immediately with the experiment with vocational groups, for which it was designed to lay the groundwork. That experiment could not be scheduled until Lent 1958. Thus I preached "Riot at Ephesus" on September 15, 1957, and then saved it, in print, for background reading for the laypersons who would be taking part in the occupational panels a few months hence.

According to the story in Acts 19, Paul and his companions get into trouble in Ephesus for attacking the worship of the goddess Diana (Artemis in Greek) as idolatry which, from their point of view, it is. The mob shouting "Great is Diana of the Ephesians!" nearly lynches them. But Paul and his friends are visitors to Ephesus. They can move on, and they do. But what if they have made some converts even among the silversmiths whose livelihood depends on the goddess? To illustrate the problem, I invent a silversmith named Philotheos, "Phil" for us, who having accepted Jesus Christ as his Lord, must now decide whether he can go on making a living fashioning little idols for the tourist trade or whether his Lord expects him to quit. And if so, what next? What about his wife, his children, his mortgage?

Shuttling between the historic and the deliberately anachronistic, we follow Phil to a moral victory—only to be reminded that God offers no safe conduct to the faithful. We are left with the painful but truthful conclusion that, however we may interpret the relevance of our faith to our daily work, if our faith leads us to defy the system, we shall be eaten alive. Just like the early Christians, but in the office, the factory, the board room rather than the arena . . .

RIOT AT EPHESUS

By John R. Bodo
Pastor
First (now Nassau) Presbyterian Church
Princeton, New Jersey
September 15, 1957

SCRIPTURE: ACTS 19:23–41

The riot was over. The wise words of the town clerk had proved effective. The crowd dispersed. To the rank and file of the silversmiths and of all the other craftsmen and businessmen of Ephesus, Jesus remained an obscure and vaguely threatening figure. They had been reassured but not enlightened. No one had risen to challenge their religious and economic system in His name.

Paul had been prevented from attending. His two helpers, Gaius and Aristarchus, had not been given a chance to state their case. And now everybody was going home, perhaps a trifle uneasy but ready to forget the whole thing. The next item on the agenda was business as usual. . . .

But there was one man in that crowd who could not forget. His name did not get into the Bible, but he was there—I know that he was there. So we shall give him a name. We shall call him PHILOTHEOS, "Lover of God," but that is too much of a mouthful, so we'll call him "PHIL" for short: PHIL OF EPHESUS. And, at no extra charge, we'll make him the twin brother of Demetrius. Why not? We may even find out that he is OUR twin brother, too. . . .

Phil was also a silversmith in Ephesus. He was a fine craftsman and an astute businessman. He had been successful enough so that now he was able to work personally only on the most challenging orders while letting his contractors and subcontractors attend to the routine work. He was a member in good standing of the guild, dependable, respected by his fellows.

Phil had heard the harangue of his brother, Demetrius, but he had not joined in the shouting because, earlier that week, something had happened to him. He had chanced into a meeting of the followers of Jesus and listened to His story as presented by a Jew called Paul. Phil had heard the Gospel, the Good News of God's Kingdom, and his heart had responded. He had accepted this Jesus as His Master and Lord. But now he wondered. He wondered what this decision would cost him—as a silversmith. . . .

Phil was a realist. He did not fail to grasp the obvious truth of Demetrius' opening gambit: "Men, you know that from this business we have our wealth." The great temple of Diana at Ephesus was one of the Seven Wonders of the World. According to tradition, gold instead of mortar had been used to join together the marble blocks of the giant octagonal structure which covered an acre and a half of ground. Silver, the most precious metal next to gold, had been just as lavishly used.

The silversmiths of Ephesus had done well at the construction of the Temple and had been doing well ever since. Thanks to the tourist trade, the demand for little silver likenesses of the Temple and of the goddess was insatiable. Anything that threatened the cult of Diana threatened the livelihood of hundreds of silversmiths as well as thousands of other workers in related trades and crafts. To this extent, Demetrius was right.

But, Phil mused on, Demetrius had not been content to point out the obvious economic implications of the Gospel for Ephesus. He had touched his fellow guild members quickly on this most sensitive point but had moved on, at once, to loftier considerations. "There is danger," Demetrius said, "not only that this trade of ours may come into disrepute but also that the Temple of the great goddess Diana may count for nothing, and that she may even be deposed from her magnificence—she whom all Asia and the whole world worship!"

Phil was no historian but he had intuition. He sensed that this was probably not the first time in history, nor the last, that patriotism and religion were being invoked on behalf of economic vested interests. Phil half-admired Demetrius for his subtle switch from the real, down-to-earth reason for his opposition to the Gospel to this noble, flag-waving defense of the great goddess Diana, private deity of the Ephesians, to whom worshipers from all over the world paid homage—directly into the pockets of the tradesmen and businessmen of Ephesus!

Phil did not know, could not know, at the time his heart responded to the claim of Jesus of Nazareth, that he was going to run such awesome risks. Religious nonconformity was one thing. Being accused of un-Ephesian activities was something else. But being classified as a person suspect both religiously and politically was almost too much to face!

For Demetrius and the guild of silversmiths had considerable power over their members. If Phil incurred their wrath, he might be warned at first—then boycotted, so that his profits would fall off—then squeezed out of business altogether. There might also be "accidents" to himself or to his employees, and social ostracism as painful as physical violence. Clearly, if Phil knew what was good for him and for his business, he would not worry too much about relating his faith in Jesus Christ to the practice of his trade. He would stifle his misgivings—and perhaps give ten percent of his earnings to the little community of Christians.

Now if Phil had been a bachelor, his dilemma might not have been so acute. At least he would have had only himself to consider. A man is more likely to make costly decisions on moral grounds if he is risking only his own neck. But Phil was a family man. He had a wife and two point two children who depended on him. Furthermore, the family had recently moved from downtown Ephesus to one of the better suburbs, because Phil felt that his wife and children deserved a healthier environment than the little apartment behind the expanding workshop. What with mortgage payments and the expense of additional and more elegant furniture, Phil could ill afford to take the kind of risk which standing up for his new faith might entail. His responsibility to his wife and children suggested extreme caution.

Then, too, Phil was a responsible employer. He estimated that, if he were forced out of business for taking a Christian stand on this matter of idolatry and profit, his employees would lose their jobs, too. Granted that they were competent workers who could probably get other jobs, the question remained whether, having been associated with a religiously and politically tainted character, they might not have a very hard time finding work. Phil did not know the Greek phrase for "guilt by association," but he was quite aware of the reality. He guessed that his younger and more highly skilled employees would probably be forgiven and hired, but he was doubtful about the chances of his older, semi-skilled and unskilled workers for whom changing jobs might be difficult, even without any added complications.

Phil was deadlocked. He could go neither forward nor backward. It seemed impossible for him to pretend that nothing had happened to him earlier that week—that the story of Jesus of Nazareth was just a beautiful, wishful tale or that the Lord, while perhaps risen, and alive, was not really concerned with how Phil was making a living. No, Phil knew even at this kindergarten stage of his faith, that Jesus cannot be kept out of any part of a man's life—that nothing is insignificant or morally neutral in His sight—that all economic, social, political actions are subject to the close and revealing scrutiny of the Master. So Phil realized that the most tempting option—going back to business as usual— was really no option at all. Having once glimpsed the truth, God's own down-to-earth Truth, in Jesus, Phil knew that he could never again live within the accepted web of lies.

The only other option seemed to be to quit. Phil thought that perhaps he could ease out of the production of silver temples and goddesses and develop instead a new line of silver tableware or other noncontroversial products. Or else he might try to make a slow, painful switch to some other entirely different occupation. But even this option proved unacceptable to Phil's new standards as a disciple of Jesus of Nazareth. Phil realized that removing himself from an immoral system would do him little good in the eyes of God if he left the system itself unchallenged. It was the system that had to go—the popular idolatry with all its phoney patriotic and religious sanctions and slogans. And there was no one outside the system who could more effectively challenge it in the name of Jesus Christ than an insider. In other words, PHIL . . .

This discovery marked a new beginning for Phil. As soon as he found out that he had to follow his new Master not by leaving behind the dangerous implications of his faith for his daily work, but by going right back to his workshop, his guild, his service club, Phil felt relieved—immensely relieved. At least he was not going to run away! With his new Master's help, he was going to try to introduce into the immoral economics of the system the moral power of the Master's life and death. For the first time in his life, Phil felt that he was in the world for a reason, for a purpose other than just surviving. For the first time, he knew a sense of calling, of real vocation—and not just as a Christian-in-general but pointedly, specifically, as a Christian craftsman, a Christian businessman, a Christian silversmith!

A second discovery followed at once. At the meeting of the Christians on the riverbank at the outskirts of town, Phil had noticed a couple of familiar faces. He had not been the only silversmith there. There had been at least two others, lesser men in the guild who right now were probably going through the same pangs of conscience. and who would probably look to him for leadership if only he would show his colors to them and take them into his confidence. What was it the Master had said? "Where two or three are gathered in my Name, there am I in the midst of them." Well, perhaps by seeking out these two fellow-silversmiths and sharing his fears and hopes with them, they might be led to discover others. Maybe there were scores of craftsmen and businessmen caught in the system of profitable idol-making, longing for release, ready to face the cost in the name of the Master who would claim their whole life—religious, economic, political—until the whole city of Ephesus felt the impact, the extraordinary impact, which a handful of transformed persons can make upon any sluggish, stagnant majority!

And there began Phil's third and greatest discovery. Suddenly he realized that all his life he had been a prisoner of fear: not of any concrete fear but of a vague, diffuse fear—fear of what people might say or think if he permitted himself just one unorthodox, unconventional move! For the sake of his business, for the sake of his good standing in his guild and club, Phil had allowed himself to become less than himself: a look-alike man leading a look-alike life! Always he had been with the majority, a chip off the huge, dull block of Ephesian respectability: prosperous and worried, gregarious and lonely, successful and futile. But now Phil saw a new horizon. It was a horizon overhung with dark, heavy clouds, but a horizon illumined even then by the brightness of the Master's promise of help and power!

Phil of Ephesus had no clearcut plan. He was just at the beginning of his pilgrimage, but he was equipped with the essentials: a heart committed to Jesus Christ; a conviction that the Master wanted him to make his witness as a silversmith in the face of assembled forces of Ephesian money-patriotism and money-religion; and a brave hope that his strength, reinforced by the strength of a tiny but growing number of sympathizers among his fellow-silversmiths, would be sufficient for the task. For the first time in his life, Phil was not paralyzed by statistics, forecasts, polls, and graphs. Now he knew that, when justice and truth are at stake, one person—or two or three—AND JESUS CHRIST—are more than a majority. . . .

Brave words, aren't they?

But I wish I knew the end of the story.

I wish I could assure you that Phil won his fight without harm to himself or his loved ones; that his business, after a few jolts, was reorganized and flourished more than ever; and that the whole city of Ephesus, purged of the goddess Diana and all her hangers-on, lived happily ever after.

But the plain truth is: I DO NOT KNOW.

Diana, and the system which fed upon her cult, vanished, to be sure. But so did Phil.

How big a part Phil played in the downfall of the system, I do not know.

Perhaps Phil barely made a dent in the system, before it caught up with him and crucified him.

But so what?

If a cross was good enough for Jesus of Nazareth, should it not be good enough for Phil of Ephesus?

Or Phil of Princeton . . .?

Amen.

Comment: Riot at Ephesus

The sermon was general enough to raise no hackles and different enough to elicit appreciative comments. Next thing, Session's Social Concerns Committee proposed that we plan a Lenten series of sermons and lay panels on "Christ, My Faith, and My Work." Session approved the plan.

After the first of the year, I secured the participation of laypersons from five callings: medicine, law, homemaking, business, and teaching. Each panel would brainstorm a sermon, with me 2–3 weeks in advance. Then, after hearing my sermon, e.g., on "Christ and the Law," the panel would appear the following Wednesday night, critiqueing the sermon and taking part in a follow-up discussion.

On one level, the response was excellent. Hardly anyone declined to serve on a panel. Most panelists showed that they had done their home work: they had read "Riot at Ephesus" and all the other biblical materials and article reprints. And the Wednesday evening sessions drew at least twice the usual midweek crowd.

On another level, the experiment revealed the disheartening biblical and theological ignorance of most of the panelists as well as of most of the questioners. It proved impossible to probe the question, "What does it mean to be a Christian at work?" with people who could not handle the prior and fundamental question, "What does it mean to be a Christian?" It might have been wiser to work with just one occupational group, leading them from "What does it mean to be a Christian?" toward specific examples of faithfulness or betrayal in their daily work. Spending more time together might also have fostered trust and candor.

In an article which appeared in the September 1958 issue of the *National Council* (of Churches) *Outlook*, I expressed some "Christian envy" of Roman Catholic laypersons who were supposed to be thoroughly catechized and whose church was supposed to offer, under the heading of moral theology, all sorts of practical guidance for Christian witness and service in various occupations. I found out subsequently that I had greatly overestimated the advantage Catholics were enjoying.

As for our Princeton experiment, initiated by "Riot at Ephesus," I wondered, wistfully, "Did any lawyer approach his next divorce case more 'pastorally' than he would have done before our series? Did any real estate dealer act more truthfully with the next 'undesirable' (read: Negro) inquirer about a 'desirable' piece of property? Did any businessman . . .?"

Most men—and more and more women—spend most of their waking hours working for a living. It is tragic that our churches have next to no guidance to offer to their members on how to relate their faith to their work. We tried something in Princeton. It did not catch on. I confess, sadly, that I did not try again.

PROTESTANT PERSPECTIVES, 1960

Context: Protestant Perspectives, 1960

I left the Princeton church in the summer of 1959. Starting that fall, I began my service as chairman of the Department of Practical Theology at San Francisco Theological Seminary, San Anselmo, California. San Anselmo's new president, Dr. Theodore A. Gill, encouraged faculty members to accept speaking invitations throughout the West in order to cement strong working relations between the churches and the seminary.

In the fall of 1960, The Rev. Wesley C. Baker, a San Anselmo alumnus and pastor of the First Presbyterian Church of San Rafael, invited me to preach in his pulpit on Reformation Sunday, October 30. It was a challenging invitation: within 48 hours, a prominent Roman Catholic, Senator John F. Kennedy, would be running for the presidency.

San Rafael is the county seat of Marin County, San Francisco's northern suburbia, one of the wealthiest counties in the nation. Predictably, the congregation would be overwhelmingly Republican. Wes Baker had been at First Church long enough to get the congregation accustomed to sermons about public issues. When I asked him whether I might refer to the forthcoming election in the sermon, strictly from a nonpartisan, religious point of view, he gave me the green light. He most likely said, "Good luck!" But he also warned me that there had been no formal discussion of "a Catholic for President" in the congregation, or even in the Session.

At this time, with the Second Vatican Council still 4–5 years away and as unimaginable as ever, Paul Blanchard's *American Freedom and Catholic Power*, published in 1948, continued to set the feeling tone for most American Protestants toward the Catholic Church. There was, to be sure, a great deal of residual nativism. But even the most thoughtful Protestants were concerned. Would a Catholic president be able to resist a greatly enlarged attack by his church on the separation of church and state? The Presbyterian General

Assembly (May 1960) acknowledged this concern, but went on to urge Presbyterians to face the possibility of a Catholic president calmly and not to "support or oppose a candidate solely because of his religious affiliation."

The sermon is based on Luke 12:16-21. The rich man thought he had it made: no more work for him, and no more change! Until God called him "Fool!" I hoped to illustrate the folly of resistance to change, when change is the very law of life. While realizing that any direct advocacy of "Catholic for President" would be misread as partisan, I thought I could use the Kennedy candidacy as just one more illustration of the need to keep an open mind toward change. I was a bit naive!

PROTESTANT PERSPECTIVES, 1960

A Sermon for Reformation Sunday
October 30, 1960
By John R. Bodo
Professor of Practical Theology
San Francisco Theological Seminary
San Anselmo, California

SCRIPTURE: LUKE 12:16–21

In one of William Saroyan's stories, there is an old man who plays the cello. He has only one string on his instrument, and on that one string he plays only one note, day after day, hour after hour. At last, his long-suffering wife musters enough courage to suggest that he might try shifting his fingers on the fingerboard from one position to another, as other cellists do. The old man gives her a disdainful smile. "Of course, other cellists shift back and forth," he grunts. "They are looking for the right place. But doggone it, woman, I've found it!"

CHANGE, THE LAW OF LIFE

The rich man in Jesus' parable seems, at first glance, to have little in common wth Saroyan's absurd cellist. We usually hear about him in terms of his trust in material wealth and his neglect of spiritual wealth. But this misplacement of values was only his minor folly. His major folly was to think that he had found the "right place" and that, having found it, he could and would hold on to it forever.

Let us not dismiss this rich man too smugly. He had a real problem. He had worked hard to achieve what he had achieved. He had looked forward to the day when his soul could take its ease, thanks to those ample goods he had stored in his barns and coffers. Then, just as he is about to begin enjoying the fruit of his labors, God speaks to him: "Fool! This very night your soul will be required of you. And these things, which you have prepared, whose will they be?"

Well, change is the law of life. We all have to die. For that reason, our personal status quo, however much we may love it, is bound to lose to that final change which death brings about. But even while our life goes on, nothing remains unchanged. Yesterday's living organisms, whether personal or social, become today's dry bones. Some may be preserved, rightly or wrongly, as relics. Most of them return to the dust, and to oblivion.

But acceptance of change as the law of life does not come naturally. It is painful, because it reminds us of our own mortality as well as of the seeming vanity of all our striving. Thus the progressives of yesterday become today's conservatives; and the progressives of today must exercise a disciplined humility, lest they turn into tomorrow's conservatives.

Reformation Sunday lends itself admirably to that form of self-examination which alone can prevent us from appearing as foolish to our children as Saroyan's cellist appeared to his wife or the rich man to his Creator. Recalling our Reformation heritage can help us cope with this time of fast, troubling change.

RELIGIOUS PERSPECTIVES

Our Reformation heritage offers us, first of all, a religious perspective. Its focus is Jesus Christ as living Lord, present Lord: not an armchair general directing his armies from some remote, safe place but a captain who camps and moves forward with his soldiers. This was the way the early Christians experienced and obeyed him. Beyond the authority of the writings which became our New Testament, they acknowledged the supreme authority of the Risen Lord, who commanded and guided His troops by His Spirit. Freedom and spontaneity, experimentation and adaptation were the order of that early day.

But the burden of freedom and the hazards of experimentation proved too great. Before long, an increasingly complex social system, presided over by a hierarchy of clergy, came to relieve Christians of the risks of living one day at a time, by trial and error, under the rule of an invisible Lord. A visible pope or emperor was so much easier to obey!

The Protestant Reformation blew like a fresh breeze through the musty halls of papal Christendom. Once again there was that Spirit-led ferment of freedom. Once again there was that vital element of experimentation, that daring commitment of human imperfection to the perfect faithfulness of a living, present Lord. But it did not last. Long before the Roman Catholic Church set forth its claim of infallibility for the pope, some of our timid, unadventurous Protestant forebears invested the Bible with a mechanical, stultifying infallibility. This produced a worship of the Bible in the place of God, just as the papacy at its worst had produced a worship of the church in the place of God.

Both of these distortions of Christian faith have been attempts to freeze the status quo, to coop up the Living Lord in a fixed structure, to prevent him from leading God's people forward, in faith and joy, into the expanding, modern world. Thus Protestants fought a foredoomed rearguard action against advances in the natural and physical sciences. Rather than acknowledging that all truth is from God, whatever its source, wherever it may lead, large segments of the church stood pat on the letter of the Bible which science could easily disprove. As a result of this futile engagement, some of the finest minds and spirits of the age were lost to the church.

And it was this same resistance to change, so profoundly un-Protestant, which caused the church to be outstripped and left behind in the striving for some of the basic social goals implied in the Gospel. For example, in Jesus Christ there are no class distinctions, but there is greater human diversity in our secular public schools than there is in our churches. Again, there are no distinctions based on race in the church according to Jesus Christ, but American Negroes have found faster and wider acceptance in the secular realms of sports and the arts than in our congregations. Once again, the Church of Jesus Christ is meant to be a reconciling fellowship where conflicts are frankly faced and fully aired. But such fellowship is more often found in Alcoholics Anonymous than in congregations where "niceness" sets the tone and no one dares to rock the boat.

POLITICAL PERSPECTIVES

Our Reformation heritage also offers us a political perspective. The Protestant Reformation was a political as well as a religious revolution. By rebelling against the excesses of papal power, Luther also set forward, by a giant stride, the rise of the new middle class over against the feudal status quo. Nor did the liberating, democratizing influence of the Reformation stop at the borders of the German states. Rather it made itself felt, in the face of severe resistance, in all the nations of Europe and, eventually, throughout the world.

It would be wonderful, of course, to be able to claim the ultimate fruits of the Protestant Reformation as the immediate effect of the work of Luther and Calvin, Zwingli, and Knox. Unfortunately, the claim would not stand up. The political implications of the Protestant ferment of freedom did not become explicit until much later, and then most fully in the new United States. It is safe to claim, though, that there would have been no John Locke, and certainly no John Witherspoon, without John Calvin!

Of course, many implications of the Reformation and of its secular counterpart, the Enlightenment, are still being resisted, even in our country. The resistance comes from many sources but chiefly from Protestants who perceive the Reformation as something for the history books and the Protestant faith as a family heirloom rather than a dynamic force at the service of the Lord of history who is *ipso facto* the Lord of change.

Thus we have been slow to grant—in fact rather than just on paper—full civil rights to ethnic minorities, and even to women who are in the majority! We are being slow to recognize a number of human rights which bear on our material life. We tend to forget that "Man shall not live by bread alone" cannot be divorced from "Give us this day our daily bread"; in other words, that everyone has a right to earn a living and a right to enjoy reasonable protection against unemployment, illness, and old age. And we have been slow to "join the human race." Our participation in the United Nations continues to be half-hearted. Economic aid to other nations ranks a poor second to military aid. And while we have ratified the international Copyright Convention, our endorsement of the International Genocide Convention is still not forthcoming.

Change—and resistance to change: these are the main items on both our religious and our political agenda; and our Reformation heritage can serve us well as a source of discerning self-criticism. But in addition to all the illustrations of change and resistance to change I have offered thus far, there is one very present issue in which religion and politics so clearly join that it cannot be passed over on Reformation Sunday, 1960. I am referring, of course, to the candidacy of a Roman Catholic for the presidency of our nation.

A CATHOLIC FOR PRESIDENT?

Let me start with a working hypothesis. Assume that the personal qualifications of all the candidates are absolutely equal. Then let me suggest that, in that case, there may be some positive advantages in electing a Roman Catholic, of either party, as president.

I hold this perhaps surprising belief for three reasons: First, Catholics in the U.S. though relative latecomers, have been remarkably successful in adapting to our way of life. The process of their assimilation has benefitted from the assistance of earlier, "older" Americans anxious to secure a single citizenship for all, regardless of religion. Thus, the wider the opportunities for participation in our society, the faster, the more thorough the Americanization. There remains only one highly symbolic barrier: the presidency. I sincerely believe that the election of a Catholic as president would bring American Catholics into full public acceptance as well as give them a growing stake in our system of government which includes, by all means the separation of church and state.

Secondly, Protestants in our country have tended to allow a number of important disagreements between Catholics and themselves on social policy to confuse their thinking about "a Catholic in the White House." I believe that the oft-voiced fear of what a Catholic president might do, just because he is Catholic, not only impeaches his integrity but casts a subtle doubt on the soundness of our constitutional system. If we got over this hurdle of fear, we might more effectively give battle to our Catholic fellow-Americans on issues of social policy on which we differ substantively.

Finally, as a frequent recipient of "hate mail," which gets promptly filed in a folder marked "Far Right," I cannot forget that there is an alliance, or at least a sizable overlap between anti-Negro, anti-Jewish, and anti-Catholic hatemongers. I believe that the election of a Catholic as president would be a powerful antidote to their sickness and would immunize multitudes against the contagion that emanates from them.

This belief of mine is just one man's opinion. The 1960 General Assembly of our Presbyterian Church adopted a so-called "social deliverance" on "The Religious Faith of Candidates," which reads as follows:

> Noting the focus of public attention on the religious faith of candidates in an election year, the 172nd General Assembly considers

> it the duty of all citizens to examine the candidates' position on important issues of public policy, including those related to the separation of Church and State; and believes that it is an act of irresponsible citizenship to support or oppose a candidate solely because of his religious affiliation.

We have come a long way, or so it seems, from the Parable of the Rich Fool. Actually, we have never been closer to the heart of the story. For the point of the story is precisely that nothing man-made is ever perfect or is designed to stay the same forever. Change is the law of life. Change and growth are the twin themes around which God has composed the symphony of human life. Of the two, change is inevitable: the very cells of our body are replaced every seven years. Growth, however, is not inevitable. Growth—in spirit, in truth, in service to God and man—comes only through the acceptance of change and the God-directed use of change.

George Bernard Shaw, with his caustic wit, proposed an epitaph for a conservative young man who, like Saroyan's cellist, had "found the right place." His epitaph, wrote Shaw, should read: "Died at thirty, buried at sixty." May God prevent us from earning such an epitaph. May God grant us grace to be, and to remain, open to change. . . .

Comment: Protestant Perspectives, 1960

I doubt whether the congregation would remember even one of the first three points of the sermon because of the fourth point, the one about "A Catholic for President," which I intended merely as one more illustration of the main point—about the need to be open to change. A number of people, led by a young woman who happened to be president of Marin County's Young Republican Club, stomped out of the church. A few members, but very few, congratulated me on my courage in raising the issue. The pastor, Wes Baker, never told me how much flak he got for inviting me and whether he had to promise never to invite me again.

There is a lesson here—about the prophet as pulpit guest. I was not proud of myself. I saw myself as a hit-and-run-driver, smashing "prophetically" into the congregation and letting the pastor pick up the pieces. I stand by what I said, but I never again preached on as fiercely controversial a subject except in my own church, with thorough preparation and an immediate opportunity for people to talk back. On the other hand, I wonder whether the pastor who, I know, agreed with me on the subject, was not perhaps a bit pleased, or even relieved, to have a pulpit guest tackle the issue. At least I brought the issue out into the open in his congregation!

Two events of the Sixties marked the end of Nativist anti-Catholicism in the United States. John F. Kennedy was elected president, but never abused his office to advance his church at the expense of any other religion. And Pope John XXIII convened and immersed in his spirit the Second Vatican Council, writing a new chapter in Catholic-Protestant and Catholic-interfaith relations. His successors have backtracked some distance, but the legacy of John XXIII and of the Council cannot be annulled.

BETWEEN FLAG-WAVING AND FLAG-BURNING

Context: Between Flag-Waving and Flag-Burning

During my sabbatical year 1965–66, which I spent in Sacramento working toward a master's degree in political science and serving as a researcher in the Legislative Reference Service of the State Assembly, there was a crisis at San Anselmo which led to the resignation of President Gill. When I returned, the seminary no longer seemed to be the same. My discipline, practical theology, also suffered. The local church, the focus of my own experience and teaching, appeared to the new "Christian radicals" as a backwater, compared to the excitement offered by civil rights marches, anti-Vietnam rallies, and the subversion of all tradition—national, academic, or familial.

By the end of 1967, I was able to leave San Anselmo, thanks to an offer of Macalester College of St. Paul, Minnesota, which invited me as chaplain and professor of religion as of January 1, 1968. Macalester College, a liberal arts school historically related to the Presbyterian Church, USA, and supported substantially by DeWitt and Lila Wallace, owners of the *Reader's Digest,* had recently received a large gift from Mrs. Frederick Weyerhauser for a Weyerhauser Memorial Chapel. Construction was about to begin. I was to be the chaplain to organize and officiate at the dedication of the new chapel. I was also to serve on the president's cabinet and in a tenured teaching position. It sounded exciting.

However, I was not sufficiently informed about the extent of student unrest on campus, led largely by self-styled "radical Christians" who had taken over the chaplaincy program unopposed by the grandfatherly retiring chaplain, abetted by the young assistant chaplain who was staying on and egging them on. Ironically, I agreed with all the major objectives of the radicals. I was opposed to the war in Vietnam. I was for civil rights. I favored efforts to make the governance of the college more democratic, to include students in faculty and administration decision-making.

Realizing now that the move from San Anselmo to Macalester was a move from the frying pan into the fire, I felt that I had to declare a position at once, if I hoped to be at all effective. Compulsory chapel had just been abolished. In its place, students now had to attend monthly "religious confrontations." For strategic reasons, being responsible for securing "confro" speakers, I scheduled myself for the first slot. By announcing the title, "Between Flag-Waving and Flag-Burning," I hoped to position myself between conventional nationalism and utopian anarchy. I did not expect to gain the affection of the radicals. I did hope to gain their respect.

While biblically informed and referring to a number of scriptural perspectives, "Between Flag-Waving and Flag-Burning" is a lecture rather than a sermon. I meant to concede most of the criticism levelled by the radicals at the status quo. I agreed with them, but not with their extremism, and I could not conscientiously endorse their methods, their style. So I chose to defend the United States as a *relatively* humane nation, especially in comparison with the USSR. And I concluded that, if pushed to a tragic choice, "I would rather wave that flag than burn it."

BETWEEN FLAG-WAVING AND FLAG-BURNING

A Convocation Sermon
By John R. Bodo
Chaplain and Professor of Religion
Macalester College
St. Paul, Minnesota
February 8, 1968

It has been suggested that, if fish could talk, they would have no word for water. This bit of whimsy is relevant to the problem I would like to discuss—the problem of patriotism.

Until recently, there was no such thing as a problem of patriotism for Americans. If you were born an American, you related to your country much as fish relate to water. There was a fishlike unself-consciousness about your identity as an American.

But today there is a problem of patriotism. The happy state of fish is a thing of the past. There is questioning—an unfishlike pastime. There is also attack—bitter and frequently violent attack—upon the social system known as the U.S.A.

Under attack from two extremes which may be described as flag-waving and flag-burning, the majority of us are restless, increasingly disturbed by the pressure which is upon us, the pressure to think new thoughts on a subject on which, up to now, there has been little critical thinking.

Why have I chosen this problem among the legion of available problems?

First of all, I believe the problem is bound to get more severe and more dangerous in the years, indeed the months, which lie ahead.

Secondly, I believe that as a naturalized citizen, an American by choice rather than by birth, my perception of the problem may be sufficiently different to offer a suitable springboard for discussion.

And finally, I believe that the problem has a religious dimension which is seldom taken with sufficient seriousness.

I. THE CONTEXT OF THE PROBLEM

Why is it difficult to be simply, unself-consciously patriotic today? What is new in the context in which we are expected to relate ourselves to the country which claims us?

In a sense, the whole world is new. The last 50 years, since the end of World War I, have witnessed social change equal to that of the previous 500 or perhaps 5,000 years. There are, however, certain factors which are peculiarly responsible for making it impossible for us to think and feel about our country in the same old way.

There is first, our rise to the status of world power—the greatest power in the world. While the United States was small and weak, the rhetoric of patriotism was lively and bombastic. Our poets and politicians talked big to make us feel big. First there was the original Puritan ideal of America as a "wilderness Zion," God's chosen land away from the wars and the sickly old age of Europe. This, then, loomed large in poetry and political oratory, until the growing number of non-English, non-Protestant people confused the picture. Then, with little noticeable embarrassment, the rhetoric switched to the theme of America as a nation destined by God to uplift, democratize and, if possible, "Christianize" (that is convert to Protestantism), the masses of nonconforming immigrants. Finally, with the expansion of America beyond her continental borders, the theme of "manifest destiny" moved into the forefront of the rhetoric of patriotism.

But none of these images—and no fresh mix of them—can possibly fit the condition of a giant nation bursting with power and groaning under the burden of responsibilities which come with power. If I have only a few sticks and stones with which to break bones, I will have to rattle them for dear life to add to my doubtful strength. But who except a maniac will rattle Nike missiles? Is it any wonder then that neither the Korean war nor the Vietnam war has given birth to a single song like *Yankee Doodle* or the *Battle Hymn of the Republic* or even *When Johnny Comes Marching Home*?

Another reason why it is so difficult to be simply, unself-consciously patriotic today is that we have suddenly become aware of a "revolution of rising expectations," not just in the rest of the world but in our own country. Our "ill-fed, ill-clad, ill-housed" one-third—or one fourth—of a nation have suddenly become visible and audible. There are millions of Americans for whom any rhetoric of patriotism is an insult, because they have little or nothing to be patriotic about. And there are hundreds of millions of non-Americans for whom America is both a dream of plenty and a mortal enemy.

But perhaps the main reason why it is so difficult to be simply, unself-consciously patriotic today is that a growing number of Americans, indeed entire segments of our population, have become disaffected with America and the so-called "American way of life," even though they are doing well, materially. We do not know the number of the disaffected. The hippie way to "drop out" is only one of many ways to express disaffection. In a sense, one may regard as a "drop-out" anyone who lives a wholly private life, without any sense of social responsibility, any identification with the weal or woe of his nation, any care beyond his own comforts. In this sense, we may even now be a nation of "drop-outs."

II. THE MEETING OF THE EXTREMES

Our concern, however, must be limited to the organized militant segments of the disaffected. I have chosen to call those of the Far Right, flag-wavers, and those of the Far Left, flag-burners. And I want to state my belief that those so-called extremes are not extremes in relation one to another but rather in relation to the middle. In other words, instead of a spectrum, we are dealing with a circle, in which the John Birch Society and the organizations of the New Left, black, or mixed, are so close to each other that their shoulders are touching, whereas the overwhelming majority of Americans, Republicans and Democrats alike, are at the opposite end, a full diameter's length from both flag-wavers and flag-burners.

To illustrate the similarities between these alleged opposites, I will offer three contentions.

My first contention is that flag-wavers and flag-burners are alike in that they are essentially nihilistic, or anarchistic, if you prefer. It does not matter that the formal goals of these groups are dissimilar, even opposite. Insofar as these goals are politically unattainable, they cannot be taken seriously; and they give rise to the impression that they are not being taken seriously even by their proponents.

If you read the *Blue Book* or any other publications of the John Birch Society, you will be able to distill, from the swirling mud, several clear social goals. The trouble is that all these goals add up to a re-creation, in fantasy, of the United States of (say) 1888—and that such a turning back of the clock is simply not a live option! And if you read the burgeoning pamphlet or underground newspaper literature of the New Left, you will find that the social goals which these people favor are made of the same fantastic stuff. The whole approach of both flag-wavers and flag-burners to the problems of our time is nihilistic, because it is all criticism, attack, disruption, without workable alternatives. And nihilism invites anarchy, and anarchy spreads a big welcome mat before the nearest dictator.

My second contention is that flag-wavers and flag-burners are alike in their commitment to destroy the institutions of our society by destroying the processes by which these institutions have been created and by which they are being continually reformed.

In California, I witnessed a number of takeovers—of city councils, of school boards, yes, and of churches—by well-organized shock troops of the Far Right. I did not happen to witness any similar attempts by the Far Left until this past Christmas, when I had a chance to attend a student conference, called Process '67, held in Cleveland under the aegis of the University Christian Movement.

The "orthodoxy" of the conference was sickeningly thick. There was one "Christian viewpoint," and no more than one, on every issue. Clichés like "establishment," "ghetto," "white power," "black power" swirled in the hotel corridors like swarms of half-crazed moths. And one evening there was an organized attempt at a real *coup d'etat* by a self-styled "radical caucus" which featured such militant rhetoric that even the hyper-permissive leaders of the conference had to fight for their lives!

But such are the tactics of both flag-wavers and flag-burners, and such is their arrogance. They know it all: therefore they are above the established processes by which we are accustomed to structuring and resolving conflict in this country.

My third contention is that the barrage of small arms fire from both flag-wavers and flag-burners represents, in large part, the outworking of psychological "hang-ups." This is where the members of the so-called Far Right and of the so-called Far Left are most alike: in their unresolved authority conflicts, which they try to resolve both by rebelling against constituted and responsible authority and by being themselves rigidly, and at times violently, authoritarian. The literature of this subject is vast and growing, but its all-time classic is still *The Authoritarian Personality* by Theodore Adorno and his colleagues. And the fact that this book dates back to 1950, and that it deals with the Nazis and anti-Semitism, does not make it any less relevant to the United States, in 1968!

III. GROUNDS FOR PATRIOTISM

Under attack from Far Right and Far Left, ill at ease about the symbols of patriotism because unsure about its substance, we wonder whether there really is anything to be patriotic about in these United States. If we seek *grounds for divorce* from this country, both the flag-wavers and the flag-burners offer a liberal supply. But what are some of the grounds for staying married? What are some of the accomplishments of America on which a responsible and mature patriotism can rightly feed?

It seems to me, first of all, that our material abundance, far from being a source of shame, should be a great source of pride for us, because of the incredible achievement in technology and economic organization which it represents. And if you believe that Communism has more to offer, or that it has as much to offer to more people, I invite you to cross the border from West Berlin into East Berlin or from Austria into Hungary.

Of course, we have a fearful agenda of unfinished business in this matter. Thanks to our prowess in production, the remaining inequities of distribution spell judgment upon us. Poverty in America is unforgivable because it is unnecessary. And the moral burden of world-wide poverty presses hardest upon our pampered, overfed nation.

Yes, the blessing of our material abundance is a relative blessing, but it is a blessing impressive enough to nourish a discerning patriotism.

In the second place, I believe that the relative success of the "melting pot" should be a source of pride and thanksgiving for us. I know the shoddy side, the bloody side, of the record as well as you do. If God willed that this continent should be a haven for Protestant Englishmen and perhaps other Northern Europeans, I strongly doubt that He also willed the fate of the Indians at their hands. Nor am I unmindful of the grudging welcome which later immigrants—Catholics and Jews from Central and Southern Europe—experienced. Nor, for that matter, am I ignorant of the history of slavery and the last hundred years of largely broken promises to the Negro.

The success has been a relative success—but as such it has been pretty remarkable. From the beginning, the law of the land has been overwhelmingly in favor of an open society and of equal justice, and the custom of the land has, with many a slip and fall, followed the law.

Of course, in the Soviet Union radical equality was established at once—on paper. But the question is: how much of that equality, of that "classless society" is a reality even now? And what was the price, in human lives, of that sudden, sweeping enactment of equality. Ten million dead? Or twenty? Or thirty?

America's experiment with a genuinely plural, genuinely open society is still young as well as achingly incomplete. But, as a relative accomplishment, it is impressive enough to nourish a discerning patriotism.

And the same may be said for the success of our experiment in religious pluralism and freedom. Again, the New England Puritans came here to find religious liberty for themselves—and they were not always friendly even to the gentle Friends. But by the time the thirteen British Colonies became a new nation, the voluntary principle in religion and the formal separation of government from organized religion had gained sufficient acceptance to become a major American contribution to the Western world of nations.

There is some unfinished business in America even in this matter of religious freedom. But it ill behooves us to shed crocodile tears about the bigotries in our past when the Soviet Union, to name only the obvious example, has just begun to achieve a working religious toleration and is still a stranger to the substance of religious liberty. Our accomplishment in this area is well-nigh absolute, and a most proper source from which to nourish a discerning patriotism.

Once again, I believe that we have every reason to be proud of our representative democracy and thankful to God for its overall success. During the nearly two centuries of our nationhood, we have experienced thirty-five peaceful changes in administration and only one major rent in the body politic. That rent, the Civil War, was of tragic proportions, to be sure. But the record of thirty-five years of peaceful successions in government is unparalleled in the history of modern nations.

It is true, if course, that the political realities of our democracy differ quite widely from the textbook model of American government. That neat model, like all well-behaved models, is one-third intention and one-third myth. But the remaining third is fact. We do have a working democracy. And I believe that the relative success of our democracy, self-serving lobbies and all, has been impressive enough to nourish a discerning patriotism.

I also believe that we have reason to be proud of the rather generous freedom which dissent enjoys in our society. The two-party system, though it creaks in many a joint, is in itself a living embodiment of our commitment to self-criticism. Likewise, that healthy irreverence for authority which is as American as doughnuts—and equally baffling to non-Americans—is a token of the high status accorded to dissent in our country.

But to hear some of our present dissenters, of both Left and Right, it may seem that dissent has been outlawed or that it is being brutally and indiscriminately suppressed. To this kind of sob-story, I respond with three questions.

First, is it not rather that we are struggling to define once again, as in all prior national crises, the proper forms and boundaries of dissent?

Secondly, is it not possible that the dissenter's cry of oppression is largely his way of saying that he has failed, or at least not yet succeeded, in persuading the government, or the electorate, to adopt his point of view?

And thirdly, before you cry too hard about the awful suppression of dissent in this country, let me ask you, "Have you ever lived under Communism? Or under Hitler? Or even in Admiral Horthy's Hungary?

There is much to be done in the United States in this matter. Many groups of people still lack an effective voice in politics. The pressures demanding conformity are powerful and subtle. But relatively speaking, America's encouragement of dissent is a sufficiently impressive success to nourish a discerning patriotism.

Finally, it seems to me that our self-restraint in foreign relations may be rightfully claimed as a source of pride and thanksgiving.

In 1848, Mexico could have become a territory of the United States. She did not. In 1898, Cuba could have become a territory of the United States. She did not. We did occupy the Philippines, that is true. But we also promised them their independence, and we kept our promise. Our record hardly justifies their accusation of imperialism with which Mao-Tse-tung inflames his people in order to keep their emotions purged and their spirits subservient.

Oh, yes, we have been guilty of a measure of "economic imperialism." This form of mischief always attends dealings between nations of grossly unequal power. But this indictment has to be balanced by giving credit for the miracles of recovery or fresh development which American economic assistance has caused to happen in many countries, for example, in West Germany.

And speaking of West Germany, I believe that the kind of peace which the United States offered to Germany, Italy, and Japan at the close of World War II was in itself a marvel of self-restraint. There was a Morgenthau Plan for Germany, but it was not used. There were no doubt similar plans for the dismantling and utter humiliation of Japan, but they did not get to first base, either. A nonvindictive peace, followed by immediate massive aid: that was the postwar strategy of this nation, while the Soviet Union raped, ravaged, and pauperized my native Hungary and all other countries and territories conquered by her armies. No wonder the flight from East Germany to West Germany assumed such proportions that a prison wall had to be built to contain it.

The American record in international relations has many blemishes, but relatively speaking, it is a record of self-restraint, with even a sprinkling of generosity, impressive enough to nourish a discerning patriotism.

IV. BIBLICAL PERSPECTIVES ON PATRIOTISM

What are some of the themes in the Bible which offer specific illumination for the problem of patriotism? Let me suggest three themes—three doctrines if you will—to illustrate what the Scriptures have to offer to Christian Americans struggling with the problems of patriotism.

First, there is the radical monotheism of the Bible, summed up in the Commandment, "I am the Lord thy God . . . thou shalt have no other gods before me." This doctrine rejects, indeed foredooms, any notion of tribalism, any notion of a "chosen people" defined in terms of special privilege.

This was the trouble with the Jews in Old Testament times. They were God's chosen people, as a people, as a nation, but they insisted on interpreting their election in tribal terms, in terms of favor rather than of mission and responsibility. It was this Jewish tribalism—nationalism if you prefer—which the great prophets had to combat. And it was this tribalism, this nationalism, which caused the downfall of the Jews as a nation.

According to the New Testament, the Jews ceased to be the chosen people, as a nation. Their place was taken by the church, the community of the followers of Jesus Christ designed to transcend and abolish all national and racial boundaries. But it is no secret that the church, before long, fell into the same kind of tribalism for which the Jews had been rebuked. The church, too, has tended to interpret its special place in God's plan as a matter of privilege rather than of special responsibility and mission. And in biblical language this is idolatry: the setting up of a particular community in the place of God. And when this is done in the name of God—which it usually is—the judgment pronounced by God's living Word is particularly severe.

It was in the name of God that Germany proceeded to "punish England" in World War I. It was in the name of an "Aryanized" God that she proceeded to exterminate the Jews and then demolish half a continent in World War II. And it is in the name of God that some of our superpatriots today would have us proceed to exterminate half the world, and incidentally incinerate ourselves—in a venture they would call "preventive war"!

The second biblical theme which, in my judgment, speaks directly to the problem of patriotism has to do with the responsibility of Christians, as a part of our response to God. To borrow Paul's lovely phrase: we are, or at least we are called to be, "coworkers with God."

This concept offers a guideline for Christians who would try to do God's will within the structures of society. For if God does not favor one nation—if neither Israel nor Hungary nor the United States is His "pet"—He still works in and through nations; and He works through persons who try to discern His will and then help to make it prevail in the affairs of nations.

Thus, as Christians, we do not regard any people as the chosen people, but we do find in our own people, in our own nation, the vehicle chosen by God for our service and witness. This is a play on the word "chosen," I admit, but it does suggest the all-important distinction between nationalism, which says in effect "my country right or wrong," and patriotism, particularly the patriotism of Christians, which says "my country, chosen by God for me and others like me, as the major arena of our service to Him and witness for Him."

For the nation is the major arena for the exercise of our responsibility as Christians, because it is the most inclusive and the most powerful community to which we belong and in which we have influence. A Christian who does not take his faith into politics, whether through one of the major parties or through any of the innumerable organizations concerned with the state of this nation, is a half-Christian at best. And half a Christian may be worse than none!

The third biblical theme which speaks directly to the problem of patriotism is that fifty-cent word, eschatology. In biblical perspective, history has a beginning and an end, and both beginning and end repose in the hands of God.

This is where the Bible is as hard on the flag-burners as it is on the flag-wavers. The flag-waver makes an idol of some mirage of the nation's golden past. Then he proceeds to beat the rest of us over the head until we bow down and worship the idol. The flag-burner, on the other hand, makes an idol of some image of the world's golden future. He forgets that perfection is truly not of this world but in the hands of God who has promised to bring it about beyond history, and only beyond history.

Of course, this modesty with respect to what we can accomplish has often been used as an alibi for doing nothing in the face of an unjust *status quo*. Christians have all too frequently fallen for or advocated a "pie-in-the-sky-by-and-by" travesty of the Gospel. But perfectionism—blueprinting the kingdom and trying to bring it in by our own sweat and strain—is equally idolatrous. The flag-wavers would either freeze the *status quo* or return to a *status quo ante* in the name of a counterfeit god. The flag-burners would substitute their pet utopia for God and then proceed, cheerfully, to demolish the achievements of 5,000 years of Judeo-Christian civilization or, at least, of 200 years of U.S. national history.

V. CONCLUSION

What, then, are the contours of a responsible and mature patriotism for Americans living in the 1960s, especially for Americans who would be informed by the Judeo-Christian faith and ethic?

In the first place, such patriotism demands of us an unambiguous and unapologetic identification with our nation—with the actual nation rather than any idealized image of the nation.

Any conscientious citizen is forever fighting the "battle of the pronouns." When Americans win half the gold medals at the Olympics or when an American spacecraft scores another "first" in the exploration of the moon, we react in the first person plural. It is *we* who have won. It is *we* who have landed that bundle of hypersensitive hardware in crater "X." But when taxes are raised or the draft is expanded, it is *they* who are robbing us, it is *they* who are interfering with our life plans and forcing us to fight their war! This tension is inevitable. We are basically selfish. It is more natural for us to ask what our country can do for us than what we can do for our country.

The time may come for anyone of us when he may be forced to conclude that this is no longer his country. The analogy of marriage and divorce again comes to mind. Emigration is a tragic possibility. But it is significant that scores of millions have migrated to the U.S. by choice, while only a few thousands have migrated away from the U.S.

Meanwhile, we are America. The government is not "they"; it is "we." Any disagreement you and I may have with the government is in the family. Resolution must be sought through the channels agreed upon by the family. And the channels can be changed, too. but only "through channels." Alternatively, there is emigration: or of course, revolution. With ten, or twenty, or thirty million dead . . .

In the second place, a responsible and mature patriotism demands that we engage in a lovers' quarrel with our country at all times. The image of a lovers' quarrel—with due credit to Robert Frost—holds loyalty and criticism in balance. If you really love your country, you will be primarily concerned with the accomplishment of specific reforms. You will also be as much concerned with the means used as with the ends in view. Therefore you will distrust the "radicals" of both Left and Right who advocate blowing up the house because of a few score termites and a couple of hornet's nests!

The image of a lovers' quarrel is valid, I believe, not only morally but tactically. If you love your country, warts and all, you may earn your surgeon's diploma and help remove some of the warts. But if you merely protest, you are pleasing only yourself. And if you pick up a scalpel and start slashing, you may draw some blood and, once again, please yourself, but you will also land in jail—or in a mental hospital!

Finally, a responsible and mature patriotism is the only effective basis for inter-nationalism. I submit that no one can be truly committed to international reconciliation and cooperation unless he is an unashamed, cheerfully quarreling lover of his own country.

I distrust men who write poems about womanhood but are unable to love one woman well. I distrust men who wave the national flag but neither know nor care who the mayor of their city is. And I distrust men who argue that, to be a citizen of the world, you must emancipate yourself from the old-fashioned, confining bias of patriotism.

At present, citizenship in mankind is not available. The only structure which comes even close to comprising and representing mankind is the United Nations Organization, an organization of nations. I am proud to be employed by an institution which has flown the United Nations flag from the very birthday of that organization. But I do not think that the U.N. flag is being flown beneath our national flag only because some superpatriot would object if it were flown above it. I think rather, that until the day when present national sovereignties are voluntarily surrendered to create a new structure, a United States of the Earth, the national flag must properly fly above the flag of the United Nations. For the objectives of global justice and global compassion are best perceived and best served by persons deeply and discriminately devoted to their own nation.

May I close on a personal note. My parents and I came to the United States not because we had decided to "divorce" Hungary but because Hungary had decided to "divorce" us. So be it: we still had some choice—and some time to choose; and we chose the United States, because there was no place we would rather go.

Twenty-seven years have passed since we landed at Hoboken, New Jersey—on a foggy, bone-chilling day—on January 7, 1941. I doubt if anyone knows of a more miserable, more unwelcoming sight than a Hoboken pier on a wet, wintry day! So I did not fall on the ground to kiss the earth. I was too cold, too confused by the unknown, too repelled by the grime and ugliness of the place. But I tell you, if I were to do it over now, I would go down on my knees, I would kiss the ground, I would at least say "Thanks!" to that God who is as surely the Lord of all nations as he is the Lord of this nation.

I am deeply distressed by what we have gotten ourselves into in Vietnam, and I have been trying, as a citizen, to help us get out of there, responsibly and honorably. I am deeply distressed by the outbreaks in Harlem and Watts, in Newark and Detroit, and everywhere. I have been trying, as a citizen, to get at their causes in various small, constructive ways.

My knowledge of these aching sores, of those painful wrongs, keeps me out of the flag-wavers' camp. But if I were pushed to a tragic choice between flag-waving and flag-burning, I would rather wave that flag than burn it.

Comment: Between Flag-Waving and Flag-Burning

As a refugee, an immigrant, a naturalized citizen, I had probably never written anything as deeply felt as this "confro" address. The problem of how to love, or even respect, a country as achingly imperfect as the USA haunts me to this day and will no doubt haunt me to the end of my days. But if I had to rewrite this lecture now, thirty years later, I would only be adding illustrations from our subsequent history; my analysis, my evaluation, and my feelings would not be any different. I would still want to be known as a *loyal critic* of my country of adoption, with equal emphasis on "loyal" and "critic."

But at Macalester College, on February 8, 1968, and in the short 18 months before my resignation, I found myself in a no-win situation. The radical students did not need me. They had their own chaplain, the assistant chaplain, who was under 30, when they claimed you could not trust anyone over 30! I was the age of their parents against whom they were actually rebelling. And as a member of the President's Cabinet I was ipso facto distrusted as an authority figure.

The majority of moderate, mostly apolitical students continued to stay away from the Chapel program, which they had long since written off as the radicals' turf. Many of them complimented me privately on the "confro" address. So did many members of the faculty and the administration, privately. They, too, were intimated by the radicals with their daily quota of "nonnegotiable demands."

For my part, I had tenure. I had never made more money in my life. But after just three semesters, I resigned—to return, gladly, to that despised political and cultural backwater, the parish! Nevertheless, I continue to wonder whether I could have somehow gotten across to the assistant chaplain and his cohorts. What would have happened if, instead of being up front about my position, I had bided my time? If I had signed as the first three "confro" speakers persons acceptable to the radicals? If I had joined them and helped them in some of their projects which I could in good conscience endorse? I do not know what would have happened, but the persistence of the questions has prevented a bad case of self-pity.

THIS UNGODLY MESS

Context: This Ungodly Mess

I stayed at Macalester College long enough to plan and take part in the dedication of the Weyerhauser Memorial Chapel, but my next call was already waiting for me. As of September 1, 1969, I would serve as pastor of San Francisco's Old First Presbyterian Church, California's oldest Protestant congregation—a historic datum which has figured prominently in the church's publicity ever since. Founded in early 1849, the congregation occupied its current building in 1912, after the dynamiting of its previous structure, in the same spot, at the time of the 1906 earthquake. Church membership had peaked at about 1,000 in the churchy Fifties. The social upheaval of the Sixties had left the church largely untouched. Presentation and discussion of any controversial public issue would be breaking fresh ground.

In 1969 I finished my third and last term as a member of Presbyterian Church's Council on Church and Society. The council's chief task was the study of public issues in the light of Christian faith, and specifically, the drafting of statements on public issues which the General Assembly might adopt as part of its annual Social Pronouncements. My membership on the council kept me informed about biblical/theological reflection on all the major political, economic and social problems of the Sixties, most of which are with us still.

Awareness of what came to be known as the Environmental Crisis had been growing in the leadership of the Presbyterian Church. In 1967, the General Assembly mandated the Council on Church and Society to study the issue. We prepared a study document, entitled "The Environmental Tragedy," for the Assembly's May 1970 meeting. I decided to use this issue for my first "prophecy" at Old First Church by preaching on it on April 12, 1970. I therefore leaked the document to the Session, noting its strictly unofficial status and explaining what a Social Pronouncement was (i.e., a snapshot of one General

Assembly's mind on a public issue) and what it was not (i.e., a papal encyclical). There was no opposition.

I found it difficult, however, to compose a sermon on the subject. Biblical materials were minimal and mostly inappropriate because the problem simply did not exist in biblical times. God's call to man to "fill the Earth and subdue it" would be poor counsel in the context of our ruthless exploitation of diminishing, nonrenewable resources. Thus I had to do what I had done in "The Right To Be A Wanted Child": I had to preach against the letter of the Bible in the spirit of the Bible or, more emphatically, in the spirit of Jesus whose counsel to the Disciples in Matthew 6 can be read, with integrity, through environmentalist glasses. I was convinced, and I still am, that we need to speak out in the spirit of Jesus even when a contemporary issue is not dealt with in the Bible, or when the letter of the Bible, applied to the issue, clashes with the spirit of Jesus.

THIS UNGODLY MESS

By John R. Bodo
Pastor
Old First Presbyterian Church
San Francisco, California
April 12, 1970

SCRIPTURE: GENESIS 1:25–31
MATTHEW 6:24–33

When the writers of our Presbyterian Church's contemporary creed, the *Confession of 1967*, were doing their work, they singled out for specific, present concern four public issues: poverty, racial injustice, the so-called sexual revolution, and war, particularly nuclear war. If the same committee or a different committee were charged with drafting a *Confession of 1970,* I am sure they would include at least one more major public issue: the *environmental crisis,* the ungodly mess we have made and are making of our stewardship of Planet Earth.

This crisis, of all crises, affects every one of us. This mess, of all messes, is within the power of each of us to help clean up. But first we have to do some hard thinking, together: as Americans, generally, and specifically, as American Christians.

To help us think more clearly, as Christians, about the mess we have made, I shall comment on four well-known biblical statements which we have been *mis*reading, much to our own peril. I shall suggest fresh readings for these four texts—readings consonant with our destiny as coworkers of God rather than suicidal destroyers of His Creation. Finally, I shall propose a short list of changes in our thinking, as Americans, which such a fresh reading of these texts calls for. . . .

I. "BE FRUITFUL AND MULTIPLY. . . ."

The first statement I am proposing for review is God's command to Man following the Creation, "Be fruitful and multiply . . .!" Even if we took these words literally as an order signed by God, we would still have a right to claim that now it is time to stop: the order has been carried out! In other words, if God created Man because He was lonely, He must be—by this time—screaming from excess of company!

But the whole Creation story is a myth, a sublime parable rather than a changeless behavioral directive. As a parable, the Creation story tells us two things—and only two things: that God is the Creator and we are His Creatures; and that God created this Earth for us. Everything else in the story has to be reviewed in light of our very different circumstances in

1970, in a world choking with people. For in *this* world of ours, "Be fruitful and multiply" is a prescription for suicide. . . .

II. ". . . FILL THE EARTH AND SUBDUE IT, AND HAVE DOMINION . . ."

Along with overpopulation, our gravest problem, of course, is the continuing uncontrolled exploitation of the resources of our planet; and the major "prooftext" to justify such exploitation has been the second half of the same text from Genesis, where God goes on to command Man to "fill the earth and subdue it, and have dominion" over the fish, the birds, the whole works.

I am not equipped to quibble about the Hebrew words for "subdue" and have "dominion," though I am sure that the text does *not* mean to suggest, let alone justify, our mindless depletion of the God-given resources of the Earth, nor the systematic pollution and uglification of our environment. I prefer to stake my case on the nature of God revealed in Jesus Christ. If God is what we, Christians, claim He is—namely, *"like Jesus"*—it is unthinkable that God should condone, let alone command, what we have been doing to our oceans, to our rivers and lakes, to our wildlife, to the very air we breathe!

According to the Genesis story, God created all things—with a place for everything and everything in its place: yes, a place for mosquitoes and a place for mosquito-eaters, a place for life and a place for death. Thus the words "subdue" and "have dominion" cannot be interpreted as religious license to exploit our physical environment, consequences be damned. Rather, the words must be interpreted as a *stewardship* command: a command to care for our God-given habitat, to maintain the web of life which sustains our life, to restrain *pride's sinful twin, greed,* which forever tempts us to rend the web, destroy our home, rob our children of their future. . . .

III. "TAKE NO THOUGHT FOR YOUR LIFE . . ."

The third statement from Scripture which I am submitting for review is Jesus' great discourse on human anxiety in relation to divine Providence. For the last hundred years or so, we have tended to ignore this entire statement as an impractical, wistful harking back to a time when life was simple—when people were still sitting around watching sparrows fall and lilies bloom. Or else, we have been *mis*using Jesus' words, "Do not be anxious about your life," as if they were a pious admonition directed at our mental attitudes rather than at our whole life style. Indeed, we have been making a Christian Scientist out of Jesus, giving His words a "mind-over-matter" cast, as if with Jesus the physical world did not count!

But this is twisting the text in order to avoid the embarrassment it might cause us! For one thing, Jesus was a thorough "materialist." He fed people. He healed people. He made people's response to each other's material needs—the "cup of cold water"—the chief criterion of their spiritual health. More important still: the discourse of Jesus about anxiety and providence begins with the warning, *"You cannot serve God and Mammon."* Who is Mammon? The god of money, the god of profit, the god of laissez-faire—consequences be damned!

No, "Do not be anxious for your life" does not mean "Be a happy hippie. . . ." It does mean, *"restrain your greed"*—and your corporation's greed, too!

IV. "SEEK FIRST GOD'S KINGDOM AND HIS RIGHTEOUSNESS . . ."

And the fourth statement I am submitting for review is part of the same discourse of Jesus, its conclusion: "But [you] seek first the kingdom of God and His righteousness. . . ." Here, again, we have been practicing an artful dodge, so that we might not be embarrassed, nor delayed by a single instant, in our scramble for the fiction of property and the illusion of power.

One way to dodge these words of our Lord is to pretend that God's Kingdom is just in the future and that, therefore, the duty of Christians is to keep their minds on Heaven regardless of their earthly lot. This has been a great text, twisted out of shape, for keeping deprived and oppressed people submissive and uncritical. During the last third of the nineteenth century, some industrial tycoons kept evangelists on their payroll to prevent the workers from organizing!

Another way to dodge these words of our Lord, "Seek first God's Kingdom and His righteousness," is to pretend that the Kingdom of God is just an internal reality, a psychospiritual something which, if we cultivate it, will help us overcome our material problems. This may be no more than the other side of the same counterfeit coin—another way to twist God's Word so that it will comfort the comfortable while leaving the afflicted in their affliction.

But these words of Jesus, "Seek first the Kingdom of God. . . .," when rightly read, actually present another *stewardship* command. They challenge our stewardship of our *neighbor.* This, after all, is the central thrust of any Christian ethic, based not only on what Jesus said but on the style in which He lived, and died. Concern for the neighbor, and for the consequences of our actions for the neighbor, is at the heart of the Christian life. It is also at the heart of the crisis, the mess, into which we have sunk, thanks to sin's sinful twins, pride and greed.

For these are the twin theological roots of our predicament as "a nation knee deep in garbage firing rockets at Mars," a nation that feeds half of its income tax to the Pentagon while failing properly to feed all of its own children, a nation with some of the most divine scenery on Earth disfigured by billboards and strip-mining, high-rises and oil slicks.

And what makes this mess truly apocalyptic is that so much of what we have wasted or are now wasting, through pride and greed, is irreplaceable; just as irreplaceable as the untold millions who have died, both overseas and within our own borders, because we did not stop to think of what we were doing—to them, to God's Earth, to ourselves and our children and grandchildren . . . !

V. THINKING NEW THOUGHTS

So here are some thoughts, no longer new, perhaps, but still largely unheeded—"un-American" in the ears of some, but profoundly Christian: thoughts we must learn both to think and to do something about, if we are to survive as a nation, as a human race. . . .

(1) Our mindless commitment to production—and to consumption for the sake of production—must be replaced by a resolute commitment to *restraint.*

(2) Our absurd notion that the pursuit of the selfish interest of each promotes the best interest of all must be replaced by the Judeo-Christian understanding of *brotherhood*—in the sense that we are our brothers' keepers, in mutual dependence and responsibility.

(3) Our brainless creed that "more" and "bigger" equal "better" must be replaced by the Christian insight that life is defined not by size or numbers but by *quality.*

(4) Our provincial, obsolete understanding of the *national interest* in terms of everexpanding markets secured for us by military alliances with Fascist dictators, must be replaced by a fresh reading of the letters U.S.—so that the letters will not read United States but *US,* all of us human beings; until the interests of all nations are subjected to the interests of the human race; until nations themselves go out of business and only humankind remains.

(5) Our self-centered concept of *history* as being mostly the present, with a mock bow toward the past and a careless wave of the hand toward the future, must be replaced by the biblical understanding of history as having its source in God and its goal in the Kingdom of God, so that we may learn to fulfill our responsibilities both to our forbears and to our children.

(6) Finally, our delusion that we must do *something* about *everything* in God's Creation must be replaced by the biblical affirmation that God is competent. The Creation story tells us that God saw what He had created and that it was "very good." It was. And it might be again, if only we learn *mostly to let it alone.*

It is not true that clocks cannot be turned back. The same hands that made them and turned them forward can turn them back. It is a matter of will, political will. We do not have to be devoured by the monsters we have created. Everything that *can* be done does not *have* to be done. Anything that has been invented or ever manufactured on a grand scale can be retired, scrapped, junked—for the sake of humankind and Planet Earth.

We are an endangered species on a deeply threatened planet, but it is not too late—least of all in this country where we can still vote. The issues dealt with in our *Confession of 1967*—poverty, the threat of nuclear war, racial injustice, and sexual identity and responsibility are major issues facing us. But so is the fate of Planet Earth, our God-given home, with its finite resources but marvelous sufficiency, if we can only restrain our greed and pride and the pride and greed of those who rule us. Amen.

Comment: This Ungodly Mess

The immediate follow-up to this sermon was the announcement of a six-week course for adults on "Our Stewardship of Planet Earth" offered by John Merrell, a member of the church. A retired civil engineer, John had headed a major Federal project which reclaimed a waste disposal area near Los Angeles, transforming it into a recreational area. The success of the project earned John an important part in midwifing the Environmental Protection Agency (EPA).

Just as important: the congregation learned that, in its Social Pronouncements, the church makes guidance available to its members and that, as Christians, they are expected to reflect and act on public issues not just as Republicans or Democrats or members of Labor or of Management but, as far as possible, as Christians.

The Environmental Crisis proved a good issue to introduce Old First Church to the social dimension of the Gospel. It was starting to make headlines. The General Assembly was just taking it up. And it was a "safe" issue on which to challenge a congregation unused to dealing with controversial public issues. "This Ungodly Mess" made it far easier for me to consider other such issues from the pulpit, hotter ones, and to do so without undue handicap.

DOES ANYTHING GO?

Context: Does Anything Go?

At the outset of my pastorate at Old First Presbyterian Church, San Francisco, in the fall of 1969, I was given a list of eleven goals which the Session wished me to help them pursue—at once. Only one of these goals pointed beyond the four walls of the church! I did what I could to help the church toward the ten other goals, but in my own mind I quietly assigned the top priority to goal #11: "to create a ministry with single young adults in the area." This might still have been a quite conventional move for a traditional church, but this was San Francisco, 1969–70, and while the church fronted on Van Ness Avenue, "Auto Row," it backed on Polk Street, the first openly gay neighborhood of the city. In other words, by authorizing a ministry with single young adults, the church had to take notice, rather late in the game, of the mounting "sexual revolution," gay and straight.

In my brief stint as chaplain at Macalester College in St. Paul, Minnesota, I had been exposed to the revolt of young people against the Victorian sexual mores preached but not necessarily practiced by their elders. I had begun to understand the sexual component of the "Don't trust anyone over thirty!" syndrome. The generation gap was real and wide.

As a member of our denomination's Council on Church and Society, I had critically reviewed the Council's report, "Sexuality and the Human Community," which the May 1970 General Assembly debated and adopted. The report was at once made available for congregational study.

In the early fall of 1970, I attended a weekend seminar for members of the helping professions sponsored by San Francisco's free-wheeling Glide Memorial Methodist Church on "The Life Style of the Homosexual." It was a minor conversion experience for me. I realized that, if we meant business about the ministry with single young adults, which we had barely begun, we would have to recognize the existence of the full spectrum of human sexuality.

We chose the date of November 8, 1970, for the sermon "Does Anything Go?" in order to maximize interest in a four-week seminar on the Sexuality Report to be conducted by the associate pastor, the Rev. Robert L. Sanders. I used two biblical passages for the sermon: selections from I Corinthians 7, a part of Paul's brief for a Christian life style for the Gentile-Christians of Corinth, the San Francisco of the Greco-Roman world; and the story of Jesus and the woman guilty of adultery.

The main purpose of the sermon was to open up the subject, to break out of the conspiracy of silence which had prevailed in the congregation, in nearly all Presbyterian congregations. I would avoid "prooftexting": defining right and wrong in sexual conduct by single texts. At the same time, I wanted to show the utmost respect for Paul's struggle with the subject while keeping him, as he indeed kept himself, clearly subordinate to the teaching and example of Jesus. I also hoped to arouse curiosity about the Presbyterian church's most recent creed, the *Confession of 1967* whose main theme, reconciliation, seemed particularly appropriate to the subject.

DOES ANYTHING GO?

By John R. Bodo
Pastor
Old First Presbyterian Church
San Francisco, California
November 8, 1970

SCRIPTURE: I CORINTHIANS 7:1–11AND 25–35
JOHN 8:1–11

If you take a nighttime stroll through North Beach or the Tenderloin, you are bound to wonder, "Does anything go?" But if you prefer to stay home, you can arrive at the same haunting question by just reading the newspapers. The sexual revolution, whatever its meaning and prospects is in full swing, and San Francisco is in its vanguard.

Last weekend I attended a symposium on "The Life Style of the Homosexual." Reading about homosexuality is one thing. Spending two full days in conversation with dozens of men and women who are admitted, articulate homosexuals, is quite another thing. Never again will I be able to talk about homosexuality as merely a "problem," a faceless abstraction. I now see faces—intelligent, questioning, caring faces. Still, throughout the symposium I was haunted by the questions, "Does anything go?"

Then, on my return to the office on Monday, I received a phone call from a young couple who wanted me to baptize their baby. It happened, however, that the mother's name was not the same as the father's. They had not bothered, not yet at any rate, to be married, but they did produce a wholly innocent and no doubt very sweet little girl, and now they wanted her baptized. Once more I asked myself, "Does anything go?"

I. GUIDELINES FROM JESUS

What guidelines can we derive from Scripture with respect to sexual conduct in an age when anything seems to go?

In the story of Jesus and the adulteress (John 8:1–11), Jesus Himself offers some guidelines—both by what He says and does and by what He does not say.

The Pharisees and the Scribes had once again laid a trap for Jesus. According to Jewish law, the woman was supposed to be put to death by stoning (Deuteronomy 22). However, in the Roman province of Palestine, only the Roman governor could pronounce the sentence of death—and under the Roman law the woman would not have been sentenced to death. Thus, whatever Jesus might say, He would be in the wrong. If He said that the woman should be stoned, He would be in effect inciting to a lynching. If He said that the woman should not be stoned, he would be showing disrespect for Moses.

Jesus took His time. He kept them waiting while drawing doodles in the sand. Finally He said, "Let him who is without sin among you be the first to throw a stone at her." There is no doubt that Jesus considered adultery as sinful—subject to moral and specifically religious judgment. But He did not consider adultery nor any sexual transgression more sinful than any other sin. In fact, He implied that the self-righteousness of the men who would have stoned the woman was a greater sin than the one she had committed.

This, too, is the thrust of Jesus' baffling words about plucking out the lusting eye and cutting off the straying hand. It is a metaphor warning against self-righteousness. It tells us that, since we all have sinful fantasies, we ought to show a measure of compassion toward those who do actual wrong. "There but for the grace of God go I!" is still the most becoming attitude for Christians toward anyone who has done wrong, whether the case involves sexual misconduct or any other form of sin.

Jesus also teaches us to place persons first, at all times. Whatever the Law might say generally, Jesus reminds us that every situation should be considered specifically, with respect to an individual human being or beings. Where the Scribes and Pharisees could only see a case for which the Law had a chapter and a verse, Jesus saw a person—in this case, a woman—a person whom God loved and wanted to reclaim. So He said to the woman, now standing alone before Him, "Neither do I condemn you. Go and do not sin again."

But bear in mind, please: Jesus did not say, "I do not condemn adultery." He said, "I do not condemn *you*." And Jesus did not add, "Go and pick up your love life where you left off." He said rather, "Go and do not sin again. . . ."

II. AND FROM PAUL

If Jesus faced conflict over how the Law should be applied to problems of sexual conduct, Paul was up against a different problem. Paul was dealing with Gentiles who had never been under the Law of Moses, and who were bringing to their new faith a bewildering variety of sexual experiences, ideals, and taboos. Jesus had left the Law of Moses intact, as a framework for personal and social morality. He had refined it, humanized it, personalized it. Above all, He held up AGAPE, self-giving love, as the commandment to both challenge and perfect all commandments. But these new Christians, these Gentile Christians needed guidance, specific guidance, for the sexual as well as the other areas of their common life. And they were looking to the Apostle for that guidance.

The first thing that strikes us in I Corinthians 7 is Paul's insistence that he is not the Lord and that, therefore, his advice does not have divine, permanent status. Again and again he says: "Remember, this is not Jesus talking but Paul." Thus, if Paul clearly states that he is not laying down new laws on sex, we can take him at his word. We do not have to accept his opinion that marriage is designed chiefly to keep us from lapsing into immorality! We do not have to accept his timetable for the end of the world, either, nor the effect of that timetable upon his whole viewpoint on change—be it marriage for the unmarried or freedom for the slave! If you were convinced that the world would end any day, literally any day, you too would probably advise your friends to straighten out their tangled lives as of now, without taking a chance on a lot of new things like marriage or revolution!

But Paul's main concern is still as valid as ever. He wanted Christians to subordinate everything to their loyalty to Jesus Christ: their sexual life, their daily work, their social status, everything. He wanted, to use his own words, to "secure your undivided devotion to the Lord." And, in the light of the imminent end, you were more likely to respond to this total challenge, if you could manage to live without, or above, sex.

Paul never meant to exalt continence or celibacy as a higher way of life. Later in his ministry, when the Return of the Lord had failed to take place, he wrote some of the most beautiful things about Christian marriage (Ephesians 5, Colossians 3), comparing the shared love of husband and wife to the love which unites the Lord with His Church. And Paul never claimed to have the last word on any moral or religious problem, sexual or other. Always he deferred to his Lord.

III. DISCIPLESHIP IN THE MIDST OF REVOLUTION

We see, then, that Jesus, while living under the Law, rejected legalism and placed persons and love above the Law, and that the Apostles, with St. Paul up front, did not frame a new law knit-to-fit for all times and places. So we are thrown back upon our own responsibility, as Christian men and women and as the Churcn of Jesus Christ today, to deal with the present sexual revolution—to define a Christian life style appropriate for living in America in the 1970s. To the question, then, "What would our Lord have us do?" I would propose three answers: FACE THE FACTS, USE OUR HEADS, HAVE A HEART.

(1) The first thing we need to do with respect to the sexual revolution is to *face some facts*. In this respect, the Report to the 1970 General Assembly, "Sexuality and the Human Community," does an admirable job. Whatever your reaction to specific portions of the Report, the Report as a whole will force your head out of the sand—and that is where most of our heads, as Christians, have been. I say, "as Christians," because as citizens, as parents, as young adults, we have long known most of these facts. But have we really faced these facts—the facts unearthed by Kinsey, the facts marshalled by Masters and Johnson—in relation to our inherited religious standard of sexual conduct? I submit that we have not. We believed, unthinkingly, that this standard, with all its assumptions and in all its details was universal, changeless, and unchangeable.

But now the facts are clamoring so loud that we must pay attention to them. We must look at the gap, the yawning gulf, which divides traditional Christian sexual morality from the way Americans in 1970 actually live and act. And this includes Christian Americans—like us!

Note, please: I am not saying that whatever many people do is bound to be right, or even partly right. I am merely saying that any moral norm which ignores actual human behavior has written its own death warrant. And one of the most stubborn facts we have to face in this respect is that we, Christians, are a minority in America's rapidly shrinking religious community in a secular, pluralistic society. Therefore, whatever else we may do, we must give up the notion that we can expect our standard, our concept of the good life, the moral life, to be forced upon our fellow-citizens by law!

(2) I also propose that we *use our heads.* We are facing problems which are simply absent from the Bible. Take the population explosion as just one striking example. Technology has made the biblical mandate "Be fruitful and multiply," not only obsolete but irresponsible, immoral. New, disturbing thoughts must be thought to come to grips with the problem of fatal overpopulation, especially in the Third World.

This same need for fresh thinking is very much present in the area labelled the "sexual revolution." For example, women have begun to raise questions about traditional male-female roles which we have been taking for granted, uncritically, as being part of the order of Creation! Another example: single persons, men and women, are getting increasingly restless, and increasingly vocal, in a society which holds up married life as the only normal condition. Single men and women are asking the church, specifically, whether they are to believe that continence is really the only morally permissible alternative to marriage. They are also asking the church, in a swelling chorus, to stop gearing nearly all church programs to couples and families!

Again, I am not saying what should be done nor agreeing with what many might be doing, just because they are many. I am simply saying that, in a world where so much is so radically new, the church ought to be the chief laboratory for "unthinkable thoughts!"

(3) Finally, I propose that we *have a heart.* The "Sexuality Report" makes much of the fact that the church is out of touch with people, so that, at least in matters of sexual conduct, "no one is listening to us." I am not so concerned that no one is listening to us. I am far more concerned that so few people are talking to us about some of their most aching, most intimate problems.

There must be millions of people in the church who would not even consider talking to a clergyman about sexual problems because, rightly or wrongly, they would expect a rebuke or, at best, an exhortation!

Similarly, millions of unchurched people are "hung up" with guilt feelings. They have rejected the old code but still feel judged by it; and there is little joy in their new freedom. And there must be millions of others who feel no guilt about any code but are merely wandering around, truculently, with brave cries of "liberation," in a landscape without signposts, without boundaries, without moral substance or meaning.

So I say, let us have a heart for people as persons and learn to listen to them, not in order to regain an audience but just to help them, because they are hurting even while they may be laughing or shouting or making a nuisance of themselves. For one thing seems certain to me: in the midst of revolutionary days, in the midst of the present sexual revolution, hardly anyone is having a good time! All of us, Christians and non-Christians, are busy judging one another, because we are trapped in all manner of self-doubt and self-rejection. But some of us, Christians, may be ready to listen and to forgive because we have heard, really heard, the forgiving Word: "Friends! Believe in the good news of the Gospel! In Jesus Christ, we are forgiven!"

Does anything go? No, not for Christians. But the exact shape of a Christian life style appropriate for this mad age, is far from clear. This is why we should start facing some facts. This is why we should stick our heads together, Christians and non-Christians, and do some really fresh study of God's Word in relation to a radically new world. And this is, of course, why we should have a heart for the victims of the sexual revolution, learning how to help them as persons, through love, by first earning their confidence as attentive, open-minded listeners.

For my part, I am frankly conservative. I still believe that the marriage of one man and one woman, under God, guided by love and aimed at having children as well as offering mutual fulfillment, is the noblest image of God's will for human life. I also believe that the most complete, the most authentic expression of human sexuality is available only within the frame work of such a marriage.

But while I believe in the continuing supremacy of this ideal, I know that we have all fallen short in one way or another. And so, as a Christian and, specifically, a churchman, I can only recommit myself to the position so beautifully stated in our *Confession of 1967:* "The Church comes under the judgment of God and invites rejection by man when it . . . withholds the compassion of Christ from those caught in the moral confusion of our time." In other words, let him who is not caught in the moral confusion of our time, let him cast that first stone—at me, or at any one of us.

Comment: Does Anything Go?

Bob Sanders' seminar on the Sexuality Report was very well received. The sexual revolution continued to be dealt with both programmatically and pastorally in our growing Young Adult Ministry led by The Rev. Glenda B. Hope, who was soon to be ordained assistant pastor. In the emerging conflict between a largely Middle American congregation and an experimentally oriented Young Adult Ministry, sexual behavior did not play an overt part. Objections centered on lesser things: the young people left the room in a mess; their music was too raucous. But what they were or might be doing in the sexual arena was clearly a major worry for many of the old-line members.

Glenda Hope moved on, after two years, into a city-wide, diversified, ecumenical ministry, which continues to this day as the San Francisco Network Ministries, an effective and widely recognized agency of compassion and empowerment in the Tenderloin. At Old First Church, Session has continued to discuss the subject, especially with reference to homosexuality. The church officially welcomes members of all sexual orientations, but has not become a "More Light" church, that is, has not openly defied the General Assembly's injunction against ordaining "self-affirming, practicing homosexuals" as deacons, elders, or ministers. The church launched and continues to support the Larkin Street Youth Center for young gays, many of them prostitutes.

Looking back on my ministry at Old First Church in 1970, when I preached "Does Anything Go?" I realize that, because of my negative experience with those Christian student radicals at Macalester College, I was probably more nervous about Glenda Hope and the Young Adult Ministry than I needed to be. True, I had to hold together a very broad spectrum of opinions and life styles. I was the prophet who had to meet the payroll. But if I could do it over, I would try harder to secure acceptance for Glenda's ministry, even if it meant losing a few more Victorian saints!

A PRESENT FOR ANGELA?

Context: A Present for Angela?

Angela Davis, a young black teacher of philosophy at UCLA and a member of the Communist Party, was arrested in 1970 on suspicion of aiding a group that killed the judge and three other persons in an attempted courtroom escape in San Rafael, Marin County, California. Believing her to be innocent but fearing that, being black, a woman, and a Communist, she might not get a fair trial, concerned citizens set up an Angela Davis Defense Fund. How this action affected the Presbyterian Church, USA, and specifically Old First Church, San Francisco, is fully reported in "A Present for Angela?"

A PRESENT FOR ANGELA?

By John R. Bodo
Pastor
Old First Presbyterian Church
San Francisco, California
June 13, 1971

**SCRIPTURE: ISAIAH 61:1–11
LUKE 4:16–21**

During the meeting of the Presbyterian General Assembly, in May, it was disclosed that our denomination had made a $10,000 gift to the Angela Davis Defense Fund. This action had done much to reveal the painful divisions which exist within our three-million member church. It has also done much, I believe, to aggravate these divisions.

The Session of our church, at its regular meeting on May 25, discussed the matter but decided, wisely, to do nothing, since news of the gift had just broken. I was away at the time but, had I been here, I would have pleaded for the same thing—no action—so that we might have the benefit of further information and reflection.

At this time, having acquainted myself with the situation, I feel obligated to speak to the subject.

I. WHAT HAPPENED?

I must begin by recapping briefly what happened.

The 1970 General Assembly created a $100,000 Emergency Fund for Legal Aid to be administered by one of its agencies, the Council on Church and Race. The money was placed in the fund from unrestricted reserves held by the National Missions Board.

Between May 1970 and May 1971, the Council on Church and Race approved a number of grants from this fund. The largest gift, $25,000, was made toward the defense of the "Black Panther 13" who were being tried in New Haven and who were acquitted just the other week. A grant of $15,000 was made to the Legal Defense Fund of the NAACP, the National Association for the Advancement of Colored People, which had secured, among other things, the landmark Supreme Court decree outlawing racially segregated public schools, in 1954. The third largest grant was the $10,000 to the Angela Davis Defense Fund.

The impulse to make this gift originated in the Session of St. Andrew's United Presbyterian Church, Marin City, a largely black church. The Session of St. Andrew's did not suggest a gift at all but simply addressed itself to "those officials responsible for Miss Davis' prosecution and all other public officials," pleading that everything possible be done "to assure that Miss Davis receives a fair trial."

The plea of the Marin City church was forwarded by our Synod's Office of Ethnic Church Affairs to the Council on Church and Race. The council, in its turn, decided to allocate $10,000 from its budget to the Angela Davis Defense Fund. By normal procedure, the money was sent from New York to the Office of Ethnic Church Affairs at our synod headquarters and, on May 14, the $10,000 was transmitted to the Angela Davis Defense Fund.

The action was duly reported to the General Assembly which began its meeting, in Rochester, New York, on May 19. It became at once the storm center of the Assembly. After extensive debate, the assembly voted to continue the Emergency Fund for Legal Aid, under the administration of the Council on Church and Race, for a three-year period, with a budget of $100,000 per year. Fresh cautions were attached to the council's mandate. Finally, the assembly voted 347 to 303 "to communicate to the Council on Church and Race its serious questions concerning the propriety of allocating $10,000" toward this objective.

This concluded the debate in the assembly, but the controversy in the church at large was just starting. Background information on the action, explanations by various leaders of our church, and reactions by Sessions and individual members make a thickening file on the desks of our clergy. I believe it is fair to say that the reactions from the church at large have been overwhelmingly negative, at least up to this date.

The latest item I received, while preparing this sermon, was a copy of a public letter addressed to our top leaders by a group of twenty prominent black clergymen who have committed themselves to REFUND the $10,000 to the Emergency Fund for Legal Aid from their own pockets, so as to "assume personal responsibility, as Black Presbyterians, for the Presbyterian grant to the Angela Davis Defense Fund."

The letter concludes with this significant paragraph:

> We need to be reassured that our friends within the Church . . . will not interpret our action in reimbursing the Fund as a signal that they can now relax and conciliate those forces which are committed to the emasculation of Black leadership. We hope that you will press an offensive, at whatever risk it may involve, that will uphold the strong position that the General Assembly and the Council on Church and Race have taken on this question and others related to racial injustice in the United States.

II. **WHY WAS THE GIFT MADE?**

This is what happened. Let us inquire now why this gift was made.

The 1970 General Assembly, in setting up the original $100,000 Emergency Fund for Legal Aid, offered three reasons:

> . . . equal justice is an unalienable right of every citizen of the United States.
>
> . . . equal justice is too frequently equated with dollar value.
>
> . . . our poor brothers and sisters are not always treated as "innocent until proven guilty" because of lack of money for bail bonds, and, in many cases, inadequate legal representation. . . .

These, bear in mind, were reasons given for setting up the Emergency Fund. The specific reason for allocating $10,000 for the defense of Angela Davis was expressed by Dr. Edler Hawkins, Chairman of the Council on Church and Race, at the General Assembly, as follows:

> . . . our sole consideration was the concern for adequate legal defense and justice for this Black woman. . . . we made the grant because we knew that this Black woman needed help in securing an adequate defense just because she is Black, and a woman, and because she, too, must be treated as "innocent until proven guilty."

The other, closely related reason for making the gift was stated, in a press release, by our synod executive, Dr. J. Davis Illingworth, and the Rev. Eugene E. Turner, director of our synod's Office of Ethnic Church Affairs. They said:

> The Angela Davis case is, in the judgment of all involved, a landmark case. Here is a person whose political views are at sharp variance with those we of the Church uphold. But as we interpret the use of the Fund—and, more basically, as we interpret the Gospel itself, we cannot limit justice to those with whom we agree, or there is no justice for any of us. The defense of Miss Davis' views is not our cause. The strong defense of her right to justice and a just trial is involved with the basic beliefs of Christian faith itself.

III. WHAT WAS RIGHT ABOUT THE ACTION?

So far I have stuck to facts. Now I would like to state my position. And I would like to begin by asking, "What was *right* about making the gift?"

In my judgment, the *impulse* behind the gift was right, even though I wholly disapprove of the action itself. The impulse strikes me as right for the following reasons.

(1) Seeking *justice* for all is the practical meaning of Christian *love.* The love which Jesus both preached and embodied was more hard-headed than soft-hearted. He knew that it was impossible to *like* everybody. When He said, "Love your enemies," He assumed, realistically, that we would have enemies. Thus any impulse to secure full justice for anyone, especially for someone who is unlovely, obnoxious, hostile, is to that extent a Christian impulse.

(2) I am convinced that black people have been, and at times still are, at a severe handicap in our legal system, so that the concept of a church-sponsored legal aid fund for black people, especially for poor Blacks, makes sense to me. I also agree that Angela Davis, just like anyone else under our laws, is "innocent until proven guilty," and that she is entitled to an adequate defense, just like anyone else.

(3) I further concur with my colleagues Hawkins, Illingworth, and Turner, that Angela Davis' political views and activities, while deeply repugnant to me, are not relevant to the case at law, and that every precaution should be taken so that her politics might not adversely affect the fair treatment under law to which she is entitled.

I say then that the impulse behind doing something to secure full justice even for Angela Davis was a good impulse, a humanly as well as theologically justifiable impulse, even though I regard the gift itself as an unfortunate, divisive, counterproductive gesture.

IV. WHAT WAS WRONG WITH THE ACTION?

So let me ask now, "What was wrong with making the gift?"

(1) In the first place, making the gift at this time prejudged not just the judge and jury who would be dealing with the case but our entire system of law. Had Angela Davis been tried and found guilty and had there been reason, at that time, to believe that justice had miscarried, a church gift to help finance an appeal would still have provoked controversy, but it would have been a great deal easier to justify. Insofar as the money was given at this time, before the trial, it inevitably struck a great many of us as an arrogant, gratuitous indictment of the court—of all our courts. For if we want even Angela Davis to be treated as innocent until proven guilty, should we not treat our courts, our whole system of law, as innocent until proven guilty—in a specific case?

(2) In the second place, making the gift from a church fund was fated to invite adverse reaction. I am personally unmoved by the argument that the Emergency Fund for Legal Aid and thus the $10,000 gift to the Angela Davis Defense Fund came from unrestricted reserves. It is good to know that no General Mission money was used for this purpose and that, in this sense, our congregation did not have any part in the gift. However, all money given to the church, whether to a local church or to a national church board, is money given by Christians, in trust, for the extension of the mission of the church; and I cannot believe that Presbyterians who would leave money to the church, even unrestricted money, would approve of this gesture.

There would have been a simple, honorable alternative. The General Assembly could have called attention to the Angela Davis case as an opportunity for Presbyterians to assist the course of justice as individuals—by making personal gifts directly to the Angela Davis Defense Fund. In this way, the church would not have implicated itself corporately. No one's conscience would have been offended. If you, as a Presbyterian, felt like making a gift to this fund, you could have done so. If you did not, you would have ignored the appeal—period.

(3) Finally, I believe that making a gift specifically for the defense of Angela Davis was a serious error and an invitation to unnecessary, bruising division within the church. I thoroughly agree with a member of our church who wrote to me: "I am not convinced that the Angela Davis Defense Fund needed this contribution. I believe that these funds could have been put to better use in the defense of minority persons who have not become a 'cause celebre' to certain segments of our population." I would add that Angela Davis, of all people, is likely to get the fairest trial in American history—if only because of her enormous notoriety!

But I am prepared to go further. Angela Davis is an avowed Communist. By her own creed, she has given up not only on our system of justice but on our country itself. To be a Communist in China or Russia is a political necessity—for survival. To be a Communist in Italy or France, where the Communist Party is just one of a number of parties, is a political option. But to be a Communist in the United States in 1971 is, above all, a political statement. It says: "I have given up on the United States. I do not believe this country can be reformed. Therefore I am committed to revolution."

No, I have not forgotten what I said a few minutes ago—that Angela Davis' political views and activities should not in any way prejudice her case. I believe that with every bone in my body. But I also believe that as Christians, with severely limited resources, we are not called upon to invest in persons and organizations committed to the destruction of our society and of our faith.

For that, too, is the issue in the present debate. The Communist position toward the Christian faith and the church is well known. I have just returned from my native Hungary—probably the freest of all Communist-governed nations. In Hungary today, the church is indeed quite free—as long as it does not engage in any youth work. For the church's role under Communism is to die out quietly.

I repeat: As Christians, we are supposed to love our enemies which clearly includes the imperative to seek full justice for them. I do not believe, however, that we are expected to finance our enemies. Angela Davis has a host of friends who share her commitment. It is their prerogative to give to her Defense Fund. As for me, I cannot conscientiously support persons or organizations dedicated to violence and, specifically, to the ultimate extinction of my faith and of my church. Thus I will continue to support black persons and black organizations who share with me the dream of Martin Luther King: "Black and white together, we shall overcome."

Let me conclude by expressing my conviction that the Angela Davis controversy may have a wholesome, invigorating effect on our United Presbyterian Church. We cannot expect the General Assembly to engage only in actions which everyone approves. If our black clergymen do not want black leadership to be emasculated, we do not want the church leadership to be emasculated. We do not want to be limited to the prayer life and the after-life with nothing to say about this conflict-ridden life.

What we do need is far more extensive participation by rank and file Presbyterians, clergymen as well as laymen, in the decision-making processes of our judicatories: our Presbyteries, our Synods, our General Assembly. If there are some in leadership positions in the Presbyterian Church who are committed to revolution rather than reform, we should be on hand to outvote them and, if necessary, to vote them out of office.

Our mandate is clear and unchanged. It is the mandate Isaiah received from the Lord—the mandate Jesus made His own as the text for His "coming-out" sermon in Nazareth:

> The Spirit of the Lord is upon me, because He has anointed me to preach good news to the poor. He has sent me to proclaim release to the captives, and recovering of sight to the blind, to set at liberty those who are oppressed, to proclaim the acceptable year of the Lord.

We may differ bitterly, passionately as to what being faithful to this mandate means in a particular instance. But if we do not give up on one another, if we keep trusting one another, the same Spirit may renew us, together, in obedience and effectiveness. . . . Amen.

Comment: A Present for Angela?

The Angela Davis controversy was the biggest storm to rock the Presbyterian Church, USA in the Seventies. Incredibly, the affair is still being used by conservative Presbyterians, represented by *The Presbyterian Layman*, as ammunition to attack any vestige of anything they indict as "liberalism" or "Social Gospel." The Presbyterian Right and Far Right claim that the denomination's loss of membership was the result of a wholesale exodus in protest against the church's gift to the Defense Fund. This claim has been thoroughly researched and disproved. All the mainstream Protestant churches began losing members in the Sixties and lost at least as many from the Left as from the Right. But the rancor aroused by the Angela Davis affair is still with us, nearly thirty years later!

"A Present for Angela?" represents my conscience as of its date. It got me and Old First Church a great deal of mostly favorable publicity. It also left me with a bitter taste and with a valuable, ego-deflating experience of the difference between what you may be saying and what your hearers may be picking up.

Aware of the explosive nature of the subject, I had arranged for an informal open forum immediately following the sermon, and I had invited Dr. John E. Turpin, an official of the San Francisco Presbytery who, I knew, favored the "present," to respond. Turpin deplored my conclusion but admitted that I had spoken appreciatively of the thinking and the intention behind the action. But agreeing to disagree does not make news. The reporter from the *San Francisco Examiner* needed conflict. So he wrapped his report around my quip that we are supposed to love our enemies but not to finance them. I got stuck with what at once became a slogan. I narrowly escaped being coopted by *The Presbyterian Layman.* My liberal friends were disappointed in me while I had to urge my conservative friends—and foes—to read or reread the sermon in order to realize that I was not one of them!

Angela Davis was, of course, found innocent of all charges. This did not seem to give rise to any penitence or even second thoughts in church members who had so vehemently condemned the church's gift to the Defense Fund. Nor did anyone seem to relent when the black clergymen replaced the $10,000 out of their own pockets. And no one seemed to care that Angela as a little girl was nearly killed in her Sunday school when some white supremacist blew up her church.

Had I been smart enough at the time to realize how my sincere criticism would be mis-heard, I would not have preached "A Present for Angela?" I would have preached a sermon to defend the action.

REASON FILES A LIBEL SUIT

Context: Reason Files a Libel Suit

Toward the end of 1971, when I preached this sermon as a pulpit guest at Princeton University, I felt depressed by our senseless war in Vietnam and its sordid background that was being revealed in the Pentagon Papers; by the horror of the prison riot in Attica, New York, and the forlorn symbolism of the Indian occupation of Alcatraz; and by the chaos in the protest movement, with whose critique of the system I sympathized but whose anarchic style I could not abide. President Robert Goheen's gracious invitation to the Princeton Chapel gave me a chance to search for the root cause of my depression. I knew that I had many fellow-sufferers among my clergy colleagues: men and women committed as I was (and still am) to the Pauline/Presbyterian "reasonable" approach to facing and solving conflicts.

While Paul's plea to the Christians in Corinth to "let all things be done decently and in order" (I Corinthians 14:40) is a reaction to their speaking in tongues, it is a clue to Paul's mind set as a man of reason, an "orderer," an organizer. In the sermon, however, I buttress my case on behalf of reason on two other texts as well. Genesis 1:1–10 shows God as creating order out of chaos, one divine "day" at a time. And in the Prologue to John's Gospel, the Evangelist interprets the Incarnation as God, who is all in all, deliberately limiting himself, taking form as a man in Jesus of Nazareth.

REASON FILES A LIBEL SUIT[1]

By John R. Bodo
Pastor
Old First Presbyterian Church
San Francisco, California
A sermon preached at the Princeton University Chapel
October 17, 1971

SCRIPTURE: GENESIS 1:1–10
I CORINTHIANS 14:26–33, 39
JOHN 1:1–5, 14–18

We no longer personify virtues in the form of ladies in Roman garb. There is still Lady Justice, blindfolded, ornamenting many courthouses. There is Lady Liberty, torch held high, gracing New York harbor. But I know of no statue representing Lady Reason—and if there were one, it would be demolished, or at least disgustingly defaced, overnight.

Reason's stock is low today. Unreason is on the offensive, reason is in flight. In fact, reason is being so grossly maligned in so many quarters that it may be in order to file a libel suit in her behalf.

THE ATTACK ON REASON

The attack on reason, in the name of emotion or freedom, is in evidence on all sides.

In politics, the enemies of reason claim to oppose the system, that is, our present governmental structure. But if you scratch a little, you find opposition not just to this system but to any system—in short, a studied preference for anarchy. The rhetoric is splendid, because it stems for the most part from understandable, aching grievances. But the notion that a highly industrialized nation of two hundred million could be governed at the grass roots, town meeting style, is absurd.

It is one thing to be impatient with our system of government because, as a child of reason, it is resistant to sudden change. But to advocate, or even wish for, the dismantling of the system in favor of no system, is to invite the vilest dictatorship, the real 1984, which follows upon any experiment in anarchy—inevitably and, as a rule, immediately. And revolutions are experiments in anarchy, trampling upon reason, inviting terror. Behind every Kerensky there is a Lenin waiting in the wings; behind every Stresemann, a Hitler.

But the attack on reason is rife in many other areas, too.

1. First published in the Princeton Seminary Bulletin, Winter 1971, pp. 61–64.

In education, for example, reason is said to have a stifling effect upon creativity. Furthermore, according to Marshall McLuhan, reason is no longer even a factor in learning, since children learn everything really important from the tube, through pictures, rather than from books and reasoned discussion. And this, we are told, is a good thing, a "freeing" thing!

In the area of sex, reason is a kind of dirty word. For reason stands for control which, in this realm, means self-control. It stands for the postponement or denial of satisfaction, because of a rational exploration of the consequences. It stands, in short, against "doing what comes naturally"—against the notion that human beings can frolic like dogs without impairing or destroying their humanity. But today behaving like dogs is supposed to be a mark of the "truly human" life.

The attack on reason has also revolutionized or, I prefer to say, pauperized the arts.

In drama, it is no longer proper to write a "well-made play"—with a beginning, middle, and an end, whether for the stage of for the screen. The brightly lit nightmare world of *Catch 22* is supposed to be the only way things are—and the only way they may be portrayed: not in any story form, ever, but as "slices of life"—raw, bleeding, and covered with flies.

In painting, the self-imposed limits of the frame have been challenged. Away with carefully reasoned and painstakingly worked out composition! Finger-painting or squirting from tubes or sloshing from buckets over any surface whatever: that is supposed to be painting fit for our age.

But it is in music that the attack on reason has reached the summit of absurdity. Music is ordered sound. Mere noise becomes music when sound is planned, reasoned, developed according to patterns of pitch, rhythm, and so forth. Thus the very notion of "chance music" is absurd, in the pristine sense of the word, which is "sense-less." But chance music is being "composed," because there seems to be no end to the flogging of reason and the celebration of chaos!

UNREASON IN THE EARLY CHURCH

In Chapter XIV of Paul's First Letter to Corinth, we have a unique portrait of chaos in the church—all in the name of freedom and emotion. The Corinthian congregation was composed largely of converts from Eastern and Greco-Roman religions. The services of many of these religions were regular orgies, with frenzied music and dance and, often, sexual license. No wonder that some of these new Christians tried to mold Christian worship into the likeness of the "worship" they knew and enjoyed—a mixture of antique Bacchanalia and old-fashioned camp meeting!

If Paul had allowed tongue-speaking to become the norm for the worship of the church, Christianity would have disappeared along with all the other ecstatic movements and cults of the day. But Paul knew that the new faith had to be built upon the old faith, the Christian faith upon the Jewish—because the

God who had appeared in Jesus of Nazareth was the same God who had revealed himself to Abraham, Isaac, and Jacob. And with this God doctrine and liturgy are paramount. For the God of the Hebrews and now of the Church of Jesus Christ is a "god not of confusion but of peace"—orderly peace!

Paul was not opposed to emotion in religion. In his argument with the Corinthians, he reminds them that he, too, had spoken in tongues, that is, experienced spiritual rapture, and that such rapture had its place. And when it comes to being for freedom, it was Paul more than anyone else who opened the door to Gentiles by deciding that Jesus did not expect the burden of the Law of Moses to be placed on the back of every man who would become his disciple.

Yes, Paul was pro-emotion and pro-freedom, but he was even more pro-reason. He believed that God wished to be worshipped with the mind as well as with the heart, because he knew that if the mind does not dictate to the heart, the result is a life both mindless and heartless.

And Paul knew that to create a community of Christians who could hold their own in a smart pagan world would require clarity of doctrine and intelligible communication of the doctrine—through the early church's major educational and evangelistic medium—the services of worship. This is why Paul came out swinging against the "Jesus freaks" in Corinth: because, instead of building up the church in the faith and bearing witness to the faith, they were simply "tripping out!"

A RIGHTFUL PLACE FOR REASON

There was a time, during the Victorian era, when our world—meaning the world of white, well-heeled Western man—seemed too smugly in order, too snobbishly rational, too blandly unaware of underlying social injustice and spiritual malaise. To inveigh against reason then would have been prophecy, courageous and perceptive. And it is true that, in our churches, there still lingers a certain Victorian aura. We could—we probably should—bend a bit more in the direction of spontaneity, both in our worship and in our church program.

But this is a different world—a world rocked and sobered by two World Wars and the spectre of a third, final war—a world in a state of "future shock," because technology has so far outstripped both politics and morality. The danger today is not stagnation but panic in the face of cataclysmic change—the yielding to unreason under unreason's attack upon reason. Thus the prophetic word today is likely to be "Think!" rather than "Pass the dynamite!"

I am for reason; partly, I am sure, because my whole background predisposes me toward reason's pursuits: toward reflection, consultation, planning, acknowledged compromise, with a deep sense of the flawed nature of man, starting with my own person. Whether you interpret human imperfection as the result of the nearness of the cave or of the ape, or, with a Christian bias, as the result of the Fall, symbol of our willful lousing up of Eden, the reading is the same: unreason is ever nearer, ever threatening to engulf us. Without self-control—which is reason's attempt to subdue unreason, we become beasts, one-dimensional brutes without past or future, enslaved to obscure instincts, lacking even the saving innocence of animals.

I am for reason, too, because I am convinced that not only great works of art but also great works of love have been wrought by reason. The impulse to create—whether a symphony or an orphanage—may be thoughtless, spontaneous, emotional. But to carry out the impulse and produce something of recognizable, lasting value—be it a symphony or an orphanage—engages the powers of reason. So I have cast my lot with the Presbyterians who believe in getting things done so that they'll last a while by doing them, in Paul's phrase, "DECENTLY AND IN ORDER."

Finally, I am for reason because I believe in God—in the God who meets us in Scripture. There, when we first meet him, he is busy creating—bringing order out of chaos. The original state of things was a mess. God could not stand it. So he said, "Let there be light!" And, starting with the division between night and day, he pushed the rule of chaos back, until he was in control.

And in the Prologue to John's Gospel, God's creative act is connected with his great redemptive act in Jesus Christ. But what is this act all about? It is about an infinite God, a formless God, who, for our sakes, takes form—human form—willingly trapping himself in mortal time and space in order to carry out our redemption according to his well-reasoned, gracious plan. Having cleaned up the original, universal mess, he now proceeds to clean up this man-made mess of ours through LOGOS, the DIVINE MIND OR REASON, lodged in the human frame of Jesus.

Just a few months ago, I stood in one of the old churches of Paris which, during the French Revolution, served as a Temple of the Goddess of Reason. That was blasphemy, of course, but the present deification of emotion or of freedom is also blasphemy. And today, what with reason being so grossly maligned, we owe it to ourselves and perhaps even to our Creator and Redeemer God to file our own libel suits on behalf of reason—in the struggle with the demonic forces of unreason.

Comment: Reason Files a Libel Suit

Any attempt at gauging the effect of this sermon would be mere guesswork. Compulsory chapel had long since been abolished at Princeton University. Student attendance was low. On the other hand, there were numerous visitors from First (now Nassau) Presbyterian Church, where I had served as Pastor from 1951 through 1959. I was delighted at this impromptu reunion. President Goheen's compliments were, I thought, both sincere and generous. And Professor Donald Macleod of Princeton Seminary, editor of the *Princeton Seminary Bulletin*, volunteered to publish the sermon in the forthcoming issue.

I would guess that, in Princeton, reason would win a libel suit hands down!

MY GRANDFATHER, THE SLAVEHOLDER

Context: My Grandfather, the Slaveholder

Within a year after the murder of Martin Luther King, a black radical named James Forman issued *A Black Manifesto* which radically altered the course of the Civil Rights Movement. Understandably embittered by the martyrdom of Dr. King and by the all-too-slow gains in redressing racial injustice, Forman and other radicals rejected the very idea of *integration* and demanded instead that the white establishment pay America's Blacks *reparations.*

This sermon begins by evoking Forman's raid on the pulpit of New York's Riverside Church on May 4, 1969, where he hoped to collect a down payment on the five hundred million dollars he was "assessing" the churches for their part in the original enslavement and continuing oppression of African Americans. Predictably, the more liberal a church was, the more likely it was to take this moral blackmail and the accompanying muscle-flexing seriously. In the Presbyterian Church, USA, many of my clergy colleagues bought into what I called, wryly, the "great white middle class guilt trip." I never did, but my concern for racial justice and my hope that "black and white *together*" we would overcome, caused me to keep the issue out of the pulpit, lest I be tagged—once again—as a racist!

In the summer of 1972, however, I could hold it in no longer. I was starting a series of sermons on the Ten Commandments. The clause which follows the Second Commandment, about how God in his jealousy (of man-made idols) would punish the children for the sins of the fathers, brought me up short. Here was a clinching prooftext for Forman, or was it? Was I really responsible for my grandfather, even if he really was a slaveholder—which mine certainly was not?

Recalling Ezekiel's explicit rejection of the doctrine of "inherited collective guilt" (Ezekiel 18:1–20) and Jesus' rebuff to the Pharisees about the man born blind (John 9), I further pointed out that the worst way to elicit a just and generous response from me was to lay a guilt trip on me. For Christians in particular, the motive for doing the just and generous thing, is thankfulness to God for his justice and generosity revealed in Jesus, the Christ.

MY GRANDFATHER, THE SLAVEHOLDER

By John R. Bodo
Pastor
Old First Presbyterian Church
San Francisco, California
June 18, 1972

SCRIPTURE: EZEKIEL 18:1–20
JOHN 9:1–4

(Text:) You shall not make yourself a graven image . . .
for I the Lord your God am a jealous God,
visiting the iniquity of the fathers upon the
children to the third and fourth generation
of those who hate me, but showing mercy to
thousands of those who love me and keep my
commandments. (Exodus 20:4–6)

On May 4, 1969, a man named James Forman strong-armed his way into the pulpit of New York's Riverside Church. A couple of weeks earlier, he had issued a *Black Manifesto* assessing the churches of our country five hundred million dollars, payable to him and his mafia, as "reparations" for injustices to the black man committed or condoned by our white churches. Now he had come to Riverside Church to collect that church's share of the blackmail.

The effect of James Forman's prophetic theatrics has since become history. His act marked the gala opening of what I choose to call the "great white middle class guilt trip" which continues to be fueled, in large part, with Christian gas.

Our denomination has been a major contributor to IFCO (Interreligious Foundation for Community Organization), the ongoing organization founded by James Forman. We also invested ten thousand dollars in the Angela Davis Defense Fund in a gesture which took a fantastic toll of our church's effective strength, and those of us who are in the clergy have learned to live with harangues about our slaveholding grandfathers and how we must pay for their sins.

Personally, those harangues turn me off. Maybe your grandfather was a slaveholder. My grandfather was just working his way out of the ghetto, in Austria-Hungary, patiently, non-violently and, so far as I can tell, without bitterness.

I am unable to feel any personal guilt about "my grandfather, the slaveholder." However, as a minister of a denomination which has been a pacesetter in the "great white middle class guilt trip," I feel that I have to deal with the substance of the argument—especially since the argument is based, blackmail and all, on the second half of the Second Commandment, where God declares that the sins of the fathers shall be visited upon their children.

What shall we make of this doctrine?

THE OLD COVENANT

In the Old Testament, under the Old Covenant, the individual was at first not clearly defined. God was dealing with the Jews as a nation, collectively. He was their God, while other nations had other gods. He was "jealous" for their worship and for their ethical obedience, because they were the Chosen People—His people. However, even in the Ten Commandments, individual accountability is affirmed. The wording of the Commandments makes it plain that they are addressed to each Jew as well as to all Jews.

But even under the Old Covenant, there was dissent from the doctrine of inherited collective accountability and its logical corollaries, collective punishment and collective reward. In the Book of Deuteronomy, the "Second Law," in which the Ten Commandments appear virtually unchanged, there is at least one unequivocal statement which flatly contradicts the doctrine. The statement reads:

> The fathers shall not be put to death for the children, nor shall the children be put to death for the fathers; every man shall be put to death for his own sin. (24:16)

But the complete demolition of the doctrine had to wait for the prophet Ezekiel who, speaking for God some two hundred years later, tore it to shreds. His impassioned defense of God's justice comes to its climax in the words:

> The son shall not suffer for the iniquity of the father, nor the father suffer for the iniquity of the son. The righteousness of the righteous shall be upon himself. The wickedness of the wicked shall be upon himself. (Ezekiel 18:20)

Thus, while the Old Covenant still had some four hundred years to go, the spectre of inherited collective accountability was laid to rest. And the spectre might have been laid to rest even earlier, had the Second Commandment been heeded in its entirety!

For what does the Second Commandment say? It says that God will punish the children of those who hate Him to the third and fourth generations, but that He will show mercy to thousands of those who love Him. In other words, there never was anything automatic, inexorable about this divine threat and promise. The punishment and the mercy cancel each other out. All that the Commandment really tells us is that our actions will have consequences for our children. It does not tie God's hands as to how He may deal with our children. That is up to Him. And to them.

THE NEW COVENANT

What about the notion of inherited accountability under the New Covenant? For Christians, the very thought that you should be penalized because your grandfather owned slaves—or even trafficked in slaves—is absurd. According to Christian faith, there is a one hundred percent inheritance tax on guilt: it simply cannot be passed on from one generation to the next, whether within the actual family, or, more far-fetched, in the ethnic or national community.

In the 9th chapter of John's Gospel, we find Jesus dealing with the problem of the man born blind. The old superstition of inherited guilt had not died. It survived among the Pharisees—and they were using it now to bait Jesus. But Jesus refused to be baited. "Don't be silly," he said to the Pharisees. "This man was not born blind, because he had sinned, nor because his parents or grandparents had sinned. He was born blind—period. Now let's see what he is willing to do about it—and then I'll see what I can do about it."

According to Jesus, then, whatever we inherit—be it blindness or absolute pitch, a missing arm or leg or an unusual gift for mathematics—is simply part of our equipment for life and of our opportunity to respond to His claim on our life.

And if we are not to be punished for our literal father's sins, we are certainly not being punished for the past sins of our nation or race.

It was fashionable, for generations, to justify black slavery on the basis of Noah's curse on his son, Ham, who was (allegedly) black. We rightly shudder at the very recollection of such stupid, self-serving, sinful misuse of the Bible. But if we refuse to "buy" the curse on Ham, we can, by equal right, refuse to "buy" the curse on Sam—Uncle Sam! And if some of our black brothers and their guilt-ridden white clergy friends insist on playing this pathetic "You are guilty, because you are a member of a guilty race or nation!" game, we can say, "Well and good: so what about all those black grandfathers who were the biggest slave traders up and down the African coast—without whom our white grandfathers could not have succeeded in their sorry, tragic business?"

A simple sense of justice recoils from the game of inherited guilt. For Christians, however, the notion that any nation or race is now being punished—or favored—by God as a nation or race is utterly absurd because, under the New Covenant, God no longer deals with nations or ethnic communities!

When God moved His covenant from the Old Israel to the New Israel, He established individual accountability once and for all. The church consists of those of us who have responded to His call, individually, through Jesus Christ. Inherited guilt is out—as is inherited virtue. If I dare not feel superior to you because my grandfather was a count, neither can you force me to feel inferior to you, because he was a man of no account.

The Gospel is for persons. Our personal response, given within our own lifetime in word and action, determines how God will deal with us. God judges us by our own faith—and no one else's; by our own works—and no one else's. As for our grandfathers—yours and mine, black and white, good or bad—let them rest in peace, in heaven or in hell!

ORIGINAL SIN AND PREDESTINATION

But, you may ask, is our inheritance of no significance then? If we do not inherit guilt, what about original sin? And what about that ancient Presbyterian bugaboo—predestination?

I believe in original sin—but original sin is quite different from inherited guilt. Original sin means that we are born, each and every one of us, with an inclination away from God and toward self-seeking, greed, and pride. In the language of Scripture, to be born sinful means little more than to be born human. It is what we do with our normally, naturally, unavoidably sinful humanity that determines our destiny under God.

In this sense, we "inherit" our sinfulness just as we inherit a general frame for our life which has been traditionally described by that forbidding mouthful, predestination. No matter who you are, you are born with certain "givens," certain physical, mental, and social assets and liabilities. You are born with perfect sight or blind; white, red, black, or yellow; male or female; to responsible or irresponsible parents; and so on and so forth. All these factors "predestine" the course of your life—up to a point. But the judgment of God is shaped on the basis of what you do with your life—beyond that point.

Yes, the sins of our fathers—as well as their virtues—do have consequences for our life.

Yes, the sins of our nation or race—or its virtues—also have consequences for our life.

The whole specific world we are born into is our "predestination"—the general framework within which we either respond to God's call or thumb our noses at Him.

As Christians, we accept these things which we cannot change, as part of our equipment for witness, in word and action, to God's loving call in Jesus Christ.

As Christians, too, we work at changing whatever we perceive needs to be changed, whether in ourselves or in our society, because "the love of Christ controls us."

JUSTICE, WITH SELF-RESPECT, FOR ALL.

And this is the practical point at which we must deal with the primitive notion of inherited collective accountability, which is being rammed down our throats today by the successors and cohorts of James Forman—black, brown, yellow, red, and "ashamed-to-be-white" white.

I have no argument with anyone who reminds me how much injustice and violence there is in our society and how we as Christians have a particular responsibility for seeking justice and peace. The question is: what best motivates people to do something about what they perceive to be right? Postponing for a moment my guess as to the best motivation, I wish to state my conviction that guilt is the worst motivation.

Being made to feel guilty brings out the very worst in us. Only super-neurotic people enjoy wallowing in guilt—and they usually manage to wallow in someone else's guilt, like yours or mine, in order to decrease their own sick, pathetic sense of guilt. I confess that I am more deeply disturbed and offended by some of my white colleagues who are leading the "great white middle class guilt trip" than I am by the excesses of black militants whose hostility comes, more becomingly, from within a black skin!

Most of us, however, do not enjoy wallowing in guilt. Thus we have been picking up one of two options: sterile anger or silent withdrawal. I am convinced that the Wallace vote has been, in large part, an expression of anger at having our noses rubbed in guilt. I know that the angry reaction—and overreaction—in our church to the Angela Davis gift has a great deal to do with the design of the gift as a gesture of atonement for the sins of our slaveholding grandfathers.

Sterile anger, then, is one option. The other, more wide-spread option, is silent withdrawal from the battle. Ages ago, it seems, there was a Civil Rights Movement. For the first time, black and white began to clasp hands. The name of the action was integration. The name of the leader was Martin Luther King. We did not kill Dr. King. One subhuman beast did it. Meanwhile, more and more of us had been singing "Black and White together, we shall overcome"—and meaning it.

But then integration went out of style. We began to be told, "Don't come over here: just give us the money." Or, in James Forman's more specific terms, "Give us five hundred million, for openers, as salve for the collective guilt you ought to feel for your grandfathers' sins!"

And now we are truly confused! Now I am supposed to feel guilty because I was held up and robbed by a black man (which I was); and my wife is supposed to feel guilty because a black man lifted her wallet (which he did). All because my grandfather was a slaveholder (which he was not)! Is it any wonder then, that a growing number of us have been silently withdrawing from the struggle for racial justice?

But withdrawal is a copout. It is as un-Christian for me, a white Christian, to withdraw from one of the major moral and social struggles of our society as it is for a black Christian to force me out by laying the grandfather trip on me. What we need to do somehow, TOGETHER, is to recover the personal dimension of the Gospel: a sense of personal worth, which has a solid foundation for white or black in God's self-giving in Jesus Christ; and a sense of personal responsibility, incumbent upon both black and white Christians, which Paul describes as our chance to be "co-workers with God!"

Black is not beautiful—and neither is white. Persons can be beautiful.

Each of us has some worth, just by being born a creature of God.

But our true worth awaits our response to His call, in Jesus Christ, to become children of God.

And when we recognize our own true and infinite worth, as children of God, we are purged of the sick need to reassure ourselves by making others feel inferior or guilty.

God loves us and saves us individually. He also holds us accountable individually. We are responsible for ourselves—for our own YES or NO response to God's call. We are also responsible for bearing witness to His saving love—by working for peace and justice, out of gratitude.

That is the best motive, the only truly Christian motive, for seeking justice and peace! I will do nothing for you, if you rub my nose in guilt—especially if it is guilt I have no reason to feel! But out of gratitude to God and in response to His love disclosed in Jesus Christ, I may do much for you and even more with you! I may even bear with you, although you keep throwing my grandfather at me!

As for the second half of the Second Commandment, the verdict is NOT GUILTY.

We are not guilty of Adam's sin; it has been wiped out by the Second Adam, Jesus Christ.

We are not guilty of our parents' sins, nor of our nation's or race's past sins.

We are guilty if we do not do all we can do NOW—to secure peace with justice for all!

But even if we fall short, which we surely do and always will, there is mercy with God.

And by His mercy, there is usually another day. . . . Amen.

Comment: My Grandfather, the Slaveholder

I preached this sermon three years after James Forman's visit to Riverside Church but only one year after the fracas about Angela Davis and just half a year after the re-election of Richard Nixon, at which time Alabama governor George Wallace polled several million votes. The gains scored by the Civil Rights Act of 1964 and the voting Rights Act of 1965 held firm, but *Black Power* and white power were farther apart than ever.

In the sermon, I tried to recapture and reaffirm the vision of Martin Luther King which, I still believe, offers the best hope for interracial reconciliation and harmony. Typically, I was too conservative for some, too liberal or even radical for others. From the standpoint of public interest, the sermon marked one of the two high points in the series on the Ten Commandments. The other peak was the Fifth Commandment, "Honor thy father and thy mother," because it dealt with the generation gap, with the agonies of parents over their strange children.

One of the things I remember most vividly about "My Grandfather, the Slaveholder" is the reaction of several members who still did not know of my Jewish ancestry, even though I had "come out" over a year earlier. If there was any shock, and latent anti-Semitism, I did not detect it. But then those who might feel that way probably would not let on to me!

THE CHOSEN PEOPLE

Context: The Chosen People

On Worldwide Communion Sunday we usually deal with relations with fellow-Christians, with historic separation and growing rapprochement within the Ecumenical Movement. On this first Sunday in October 1974, however, I decided to address the problem of Jewish-Christian relations—for the first time in my 32 years as a minister. The very fact that I waited so long shows how ill at ease I was about addressing the subject.

I had broken my silence about our Jewish background three years earlier. Father, who had somehow managed to keep the skeleton closeted, was dead. Mother felt that I should have let well enough alone. For me, "coming out" was a relief, and I knew that, before long, I would want to deal with the issue in the pulpit.

The problem of Jewish-Christian relations is of course as old as the Christian church. Christianity began as a movement within Judaism. The earliest Christians, including Jesus himself, were Jews. But the majority of Jews would not accept Jesus as the promised Messiah. They resisted the church's proselyting efforts. Paul, himself a convert from the strictest Judaism, agonized over the problem of the "specialness" of the Jews from the standpoint of the Christian evangelistic imperative (Romans 9 through 11).

But Paul's wistful love for his people did not set the tone for the church. By the time Christianity became the official religion of the Roman Empire, the church's doctrine was set: the Jews must be converted, *or else*. . . . The subsequent centuries are a history of that "or else," which includes the Holocaust perpetrated by a nominally Christian nation.

The Organizing Assembly of the World Council of Churches (Amsterdam, 1948), which I attended as an interpreter, had a unique opportunity to break fresh ground, to begin questioning, with Paul, the need to evangelize the Jews. The Holocaust might have at least triggered some fresh thinking on the subject. But it did not. The report, *The Christian Approach to the Jews*, expressed penitence about the Holocaust and included a section on "The Special Meaning of the Jewish People for Christian Faith," but reaffirmed the church's commitment to Jewish evangelism both through special agencies and "as a normal part of parish work." Subsequent statements by churches, like the Vatican's *Nostra Aetate* (1965) echoed the same doctrine.

"The Chosen People" does not break any fresh ground, either. It does present, conscientiously, Paul's dilemma and ours, a dilemma rendered wholly unmanageable by the Holocaust. In working on the sermon, I wondered whether I should inject my own story as a Jewish-Christian at all. I decided against doing so; the people of Old First Church, who knew the story could draw their own conclusions. Whatever the sermon might mean to them, writing it proved an important part of my continuing formation as a Jewish-Christian minister.

THE CHOSEN PEOPLE

By John R. Bodo
Pastor
Old First Presbyterian Church
San Francisco, California
October 6, 1974

SCRIPTURE: ROMANS 9:1–5
ROMANS 11:13–18

No people in history has suffered more nor survived more stubbornly than the Jews. Jewish humor often reflects the horror and tragedy of Jewish suffering and the indomitable courage of our Lord's people. Take the heart-rending joke about the old German Jew praying in a concentration camp: "O God of Abraham, God of Isaac, God of Jacob: we have been Thy chosen people for lo! these five thousand years. *Please* choose now another!"

The Chosen People! However we may interpret the expression, it has an immediate basic credibility. The mere fact that there are any Jews left in the world seems proof enough of a special destiny. Such powers of survival are beyond human comprehension except as a part of some special design of God.

Moreover, the amount and caliber of human genius which this small people has contributed to the race is further testimony to their uniqueness. We need to think of just three men: Karl Marx, the disturber of our social universe; Sigmund Freud, the disturber of our psychic universe; and Albert Einstein, the disturber of our physical universe. However we may feel about their particular contributions, these men *are* the twentieth century.

A CHRISTIAN VIEW OF THE JEWS

So the Jews are, somehow, the Chosen People. What then? How shall we, as Christians, interpret the meaning and significance of this statement?

For one thing, we must remember that, in our faith, we are inseparably linked with the Jews. Our Christian faith is rooted in the Hebrew faith. Even Paul, than whom no one drew a sharper line between the Old Covenant and the New Covenant, unequivocally affirmed our close kinship with the Jews. A convert from the strictest Judaism, Paul agonized over the problem of his fellow-Jews who were unable to acknowledge Jesus as the promised Messiah.

"I could wish that I myself were accursed and cut off for the sake of my brethren," Paul wrote to the Christians at Rome. "They are Israelites, and to them belong the sonship, the glory, the covenants, the giving of the Law, the worship, and the promises; to them belong the partiarchs; and of their race, according to the flesh, is the Christ."

This is something we can never forget: that when God saw fit to become Man, He did not become a Roman, nor a Gentile-American, but a Jew. Every time I see Sallman's "Head of Christ," that bearded version of a fair-skinned, sentimentalized Superman, I am repelled by the historic, artistic, and theological blasphemy!

Yes, Jesus was a Jew: a plain, devout Jew. He was plain because He was born into a humble, Jewish home. He was devout because He absorbed from His parents a simple, profound Jewish devotion from which, to the end of his days, He never swerved. In His early instructions to the Disciples, Jesus informed them that their mission was to "the lost sheep of Israel," and no one else. Only later did he redraw the boundaries of their mission to encompass the whole human race. He was a Jew to the end. His tears of sorrow at the sight of Jerusalem, the city He so deeply loved, the city where He would be crucified, are further proof of His deep roots in His people. No wonder that all the Disciples/Apostles were Jews. No wonder that all the books of the New Testament, with the exception of Luke's Gospel and his history of the Apostles, were written by Jewish Christians. . . .

But what about the Jews who did not become Christians? Paul had some of his toughest battles with them. At times he was at his wits' end and wrote bitter things about them. But his most revealing passage, the one most in accord with the inspired visions of Isaiah and others, is a hymn of hope. Writing to Gentile-Christians in Rome, Paul asks: "Has God rejected His people?" And his answer is "By no means!" Then, in prose which borders on poetry, Paul compares God's people to an olive tree. He writes: "If the root is holy, so are the branches. But if some of the branches were broken off, and you (Gentiles), a wild olive shoot, were grafted in their place to share the richness of the olive tree, do not boast over the branches. If you boast, remember: it is not you that support the root, but the root that supports you."

Here, then is the paradox: as Christians, we are inseparably linked with the Jews as well as decisively divided from them. We belong together not only as members of the human race but, more profoundly, through Abraham, Moses, the prophets, and—supremely—through Jesus and the Apostles. At the same time, we are set apart, sharply, dramatically, by that fundamental conviction of Christians which the majority of Jews have been unable to accept: the identity of Jesus of Nazareth with the promised Messiah, the Son of God, the Saviour. . . .

PROBLEMS FOR CHRISTIANS

The paradox perplexes us on three major fronts.

We are perplexed, first of all, by the question: what really are the Jews? A race? But race is a fiction. It presupposes distinct physical characteristics uniformly present in all members of the group. In this sense, Jews are no more a race than Americans are a race.

Are they a nation then? We know that they were a nation until the year 70 A.D. when the Romans put a bloody end to their nationhood. We also know that, nearly nineteen centuries later, in 1948, a new Jewish state emerged from the struggles of a handful of dauntless pioneers and the blunders of several confused governments. But the nation of Israel is no more than a symbol: inspiring to some, irritating to others. It is a symbol of unquenchable Jewish vitality, but beyond this obvious meaning, the symbol is quite blurred. Most of the world's Jews do not live in Israel, nor do they desire to live there. Some are deeply interested in Israel, others are indifferent, still others are antagonistic. Meanwhile, they are citizens of their own nations, by birth or adoption—assimilated and loyal.

Not a race, not a nation . . . A religion, then? To be sure, the religion of what we call the Old Testament and the religious thought and devotion of later interpreters, sages, mystics, have been the most powerful bond among Jews. But today, especially in free countries like ours but even in Israel, many Jews do not practice Judaism while regarding themselves as Jews just as surely!

In short, there is no clear-cut answer to the question of Jewish identity. Living all over the world, bound together by a strong but elusive bond, the Jews are not a race; they are more than a nation; they are more than a religious community. What they are escapes all our neat little pigeonholes unless we remember that, somehow, they are the Chosen People. . . .

But this brings up another perplexing problem. According to Paul, the Christian church has replaced the Jews as God's Chosen People. The church is the New Israel, supplanting and fulfilling the Old. Having found the promised Messiah in Jesus, it is our mission now to continue the mission of the Apostles, the conversion of all humankind to the Christian faith; and this missionary mandate surely includes the conversion of the Jews. Or does it? And if so, how shall we go about it?

Our spirits are heavy with the memory of the misdeeds of our Christian ancestors who tried to "convert" Jews at sword's point, on the rack, or at the stake. And when they would not be "converted," our Christian ancestors sealed off the Jews in ghettoes, restricting them to the most despised occupations—like money-lending, inflicting on them a crushing ostracism, which they could only escape if they betrayed their faith. How can we ever live down these ancient indignities and their far more horrible, twentieth-century extensions—like the Holocaust? How can we ever inspire in our Jewish neighbors a sense of trust which would enable them to see beyond us—to Jesus, the Christ—whom we would share with them?

For this is our third and most perplexing problem: we cannot escape the sense of collective guilt for the persecution, the oppression, the attempted extermination of the Jews—from the earliest Christian centuries to the century which has produced Majdanek and Treblinka and Auschwitz.

It is this sense of guilt which makes some of us wish that the Jews, all the Jews, would somehow become a nation, in Israel or almost anywhere, so that we could at last define them and, having defined them, wash our conscience of them. The same sense of guilt that makes others wish that, by some miracle, all Jews might be converted, in other words, conform and disappear, so that we would be rid of the "Jewish problem." But our conscience does not let us off the hook. We know that our government had every opportunity to save Europe's Jews, or at least most of them, but not enough of us cared. We know that anti-Semitism to this day is just barely beneath the surface—and that it frequently surfaces, as it has in the monstrous lies of self-styled American "historians" who tell us that there was no Holocaust! We know, in short, that there is no "Jewish problem," only a Gentile problem—a Gentile-Christian problem.

TOWARD A SOLUTION

Is there a solution?

I believe that there is, but that its time and conditions are buried deep in the mind of God. There are, however, certain things which we Christians can do to prepare the way.

For one thing, as American Christians, we can stop pretending that America is a "Christian country." There is no Christian country. There are only Christian persons, and their names and number are known only to God. As for America, ours is a nation whose history, political structures and moral ideals have been deeply influenced by the Judeo-Christian religion and ethic. Historically, culturally, religiously, Jews are as indigenous to our nation as Christians are. We may well recall that our Jewish fellow-Americans celebrated their 300th anniversary in America in 1954.

We also need to realize that the majority of Americans are neither Jews nor Christians, but "Gentiles": religiously uncommitted, uninformed, uncaring. The sooner we accept these facts about our country—that we are not a "Christian nation" either historically or statistically—the easier it will be for us to accept our Jewish fellow-citizens, simply as fellow-Americans, without any sense of strangeness—on the same, broad, human basis on which we accept most of our neighbors and friends who are Gentiles, that is, non-Jewish, non-Christian Americans.

Another thing we can do as American Christians is to realize that freedom is all of one piece. We did not prevent Hitler from killing first Jews, then Poles, then Dutchmen, Frenchmen, and Englishmen. We allowed Hitler to forge ahead, dividing and conquering, until he was killing Americans. Had we realized that freedom is indivisible, had we rescued the Jews of Europe, we might not have been forced to defend ourselves at the cost of billions of dollars and tens of thousands of American casualties. As long as we keep pretending that freedom is a right for us and a privilege for others, we will remain under God's judgment. This has been painfully obvious in the historic consequences of our withholding and, to this day, stinting, the freedom of black people. It is less obvious but still present in our careless toleration of anti-Semitism.

Still another thing we can do is to get to know each other better. Instead of treating Judaism as a mere prelude to Christianity, we need to explore at least four vistas of the "Jewish problem" as essentially a Christian problem: our respective understandings of what God's Word is and in what sense it is God's Word; anti-Semitism—as a Christian invention; Judaism as a living faith; and the significance of Israel. Yes, we need to find out a great deal more about the Jewish faith, about Jewish culture, yes, and about Jewish suffering, especially about the Holocaust which we have been trying to ignore.

But are we not begging the basic question, the haunting, inescapable question, about Jesus the Christ—the Son of Man who wept over Jerusalem—the Son of God whose Spirit surely longs to win all people to Himself, including His own people?

Yes, this is the basic question, but I do not have the answer. This is the fundamental problem for Christians in relation to Jews, but I do not have the solution. In addition to what has already been said, however, I can submit two further personal convictions.

The first conviction is that the only valid missionary approach to the Jews is by example. Argument is unavailing. Even Paul never argued anyone into believing. The witness of his life argued for him. After all, the witness of a life transformed by the love and power of Jesus Christ has always been the most potent evangelistic argument.

But this conviction may be too general. It does indeed apply to the Christian approach not only to Jews but to any and all non-Christians. So let me make my second conviction more specific. It is this: Jews are so slow to respond to our evangelistic or missionary efforts because they know us too well. They would not respond when our ancestors tortured and burned them in order to "save their souls." But if they remained unimpressed by violence, they will not be impressed by our halfway, half-hearted Christianity, either. Of all the people in the world who depend on us for a saving knowledge of the love and power of our Lord, the Jews are the most demanding. They will accept Jesus as their Savior if we can show them, not just by words but by our whole life, individual and collective, that we have accepted Him as our Master. . . . Amen.

Comment: The Chosen People

I missed an important opportunity on October 6, 1974, when I failed to plan a follow-up session for "The Chosen People." I was exhausted from our elaborate, January-through-May celebration of the 125th anniversary of the "oldest Protestant church in California." Too, Mary and I had just been married, which required moving and all sorts of other adjustments. So I preached, shook hands at the door, and went home, as frustrated as ever about the church's formal (though mostly ineffectual) commitment to evangelize Jews.

For the record, though, something truly significant happened thirteen years later. The Presbyterian General Assembly of 1987 adopted a statement entitled, cumbersomely, *A Theological Understanding of the Relationship Between Christians and Jews.* The statement boldly lays to rest the very idea of Jewish evangelism. Comprising seven "Affirmations and Explications," the statement affirms: (1) The God we worship is the same God. (2) Christians have not replaced ("superseded") Jews as God's "true Israel." (3) Both Jews and Christians "are elected by God for witness to the world." (4) Jews are "in a covenantal relationship with God," just as we are. (5) We repent of anti-Semitism fueled by the church's "teaching of contempt" for the Jews. (6) We acknowledge God's promise of land to God's people, but we define "land" not as "a specific geographical entity" but as "sustainable life, prosperity, peace and security." (7) We are "partners in waiting. . . . together we await . . . (God's) peaceable kingdom."

As a "study document" commended to its member churches by the governing body of a single denomination, this truly revolutionary statement received hardly any notice—partly because of its lowly status, largely because of its subject: Jewish evangelism, is just not an issue—at least in our mainstream churches. Small numbers of Jews do become Protestants or Catholics through intermarriage, though few of them ever become active in their congregations. Specific efforts at converting Jews are still being made by some Fundamentalist denominations and by special communities like Jews for Jesus.

The statement of the 1987 Presbyterian General Assembly is being used, effectively, in Jewish-Christian dialogues which, more recently, have come to include Buddhists and/or Muslims, making them truly interfaith conversations. In our increasingly multicultural society, these small ripples may be heralds of a wave of the future.

WHO NEEDS WOMEN'S LIB?

Context: Who Needs Women's Lib?

It took the women of this nation three quarters of a century to secure the franchise. The struggle for genuine equality under the law and in the market place has gone on for at least as long, and victory is not yet in sight; in fact, the hope, which surged around the proposed Equal Rights Amendment (ERA) in the Seventies and early Eighties, abated with the failure of the amendment to be adopted by the requisite number of states.

I preached "Who Needs Women's Lib?" when the movement seemed to be making solid progress against mounting stand-patter resistance (by Phyllis Schlafly *et al.*) and when hope for the passage of the ERA was running high. I expected and received a mostly sympathetic hearing from the Old First congregation. I believe that it was worth their time, though, to have the issue of sexism presented in a biblical/theological framework. For that matter, the very word "sexism" grated on many ears and needed to be understood and assimilated.

As in most mainstream Protestant congregations, women outnumbered men in the church at least 2 to 1. There was no problem about the acceptance of women as deacons or even as elders. Between one-third and one-half of the elders/trustees were women. Many old-timers, however, had strongly opposed the ministry of Glenda Hope, not just because of whatever she did but because who she was: a woman minister. Sexism was alive and well in Old First Church of San Francisco.

In 1975, hardly any of the currently married women in the church held outside jobs. Employed singles, many of them underemployed, most of them underpaid, would sympathize with my description of sexism in action. But even some of them would uphold woman as homemaker as the Christian ideal. They would also feel that Women's Lib is about and for someone else, and they would loudly disapprove bra-burning!

WHO NEEDS WOMEN'S LIB?

By John R. Bodo
Pastor
Old First Presbyterian Church
San Francisco, California
April 20, 1975

SCRIPTURE: GENESIS 1:26–28
GALATIANS 3:27–29
LUKE 15:8–10

I know that among church people there is a wide gamut of opinion not just about the Equal Rights Amendment but about the equal rights for women movement often referred to as "Women's Lib." While some of us warmly endorse our Presbyterian Church's support of the movement, others are asking in sincere perplexity, "Who needs Women's Lib?" Still others rephrase the question with open hostility, "Women's Lib: who needs it?"

RIGHTING SOME WRONGS

It is true that there were at first some truly annoying excesses, like bra-burning, which gave the very phrase "Women's Lib" an unpleasant ring. But these excesses were few and marginal, irrelevant to what the women's rights movement is fundamentally all about.

The women's rights movement is not about bras or other trivia. It is, first of all, about equal rights for women under law because, at this juncture, women are nowhere near equal under our laws. American law is grounded in English common law in which, according to the eminent eighteenth-century English jurist, Blackstone, "when a man and a woman get married, they become one, and that 'one' is the husband."

Let me offer a few examples of how this discrimination operates in our state laws; and, remember, in the absence of any specific protection of women's rights in the Federal Constitution, state law rules—fifty sets of state laws.

In Arkansas, all personal property, including household furnishings, belong to the husband. The wife can only claim anything if she files a statement with the county recorder proving that she had purchased the item with her own outside earnings. Her unpaid labor as a homemaker is not recognized either in Arkansas, or in most other states.

In Vermont, the double standard is equally clear. When a husband is granted a divorce because of his wife's adultery, he may be granted all the property, including property owned separately in her name. But if a wife is granted a divorce because of her husband's adultery, she has no claim to his separately owned property.

In Georgia, a woman can buy a house, but her husband can sell it without even telling her. The Georgia Code echoes Blackstone's eighteenth-century statement almost literally when it states that "the husband is the head of the family and the wife is subject to him, her legal existence is merged in the husband. . . ." (Georgia Code, ANN., 53–501, 1974)

Without specific protection under the Federal Constitution, such as the Equal Rights Amendment proposes, there is no national standard for the rights of women under the law. As a result, women at present have few weapons for challenging flagrant discrimination in the economy.

The most widely publicized and most convicting statistic about the unequal treatment of women in our economy is that women earn only 59 cents for every dollar men earn. Not only can't women get equal pay for equal work, they can't get equal work. Seventy-five percent of all employed women are in pink-collar jobs—as secretaries, maids, waitresses, beauticians. And if you, a well-employed woman, are an exception, with your college education and your big, lucrative job, consider that you are truly an exception. Only 1 percent of women hold top jobs in business and industry. And of all people who earn over $25,000 a year, only three-tenths of one percent are women.

This is what the women's rights movement is all about! Not about bras. Not about integrating public bathrooms. Not about any of the red herrings which Phyllis Schlafly and her ilk peddle. The women's rights movement is about equal justice for 51 percent of Americans, under law and in the marketplace!

Underlying all the specific instances of discrimination and exploitation and all the specific remedies sought, including ERA, the women's rights movement is fundamentally about sexism.

What is the meaning of this strange, fighting word, "sexism"? The best way I know to explain it is to compare it to its twin, racism. Racism is the assumption that all members of a race are alike. All the assumptions within this basic assumption are not necessarily derogatory. Far from it! Sure, if you are Black, you are supposed to be lazy, happy-go-lucky, messy—all unflattering attributes. But you are also supposed to have rhythm, and enormous sexual powers—two highly flattering stereotypes! What matters, though, is that both kinds of assumptions, both kinds of stereotypes, unflattering and flattering, are putdowns, because they deal with you as a faceless member of a group, all of whose members are assumed to be alike!

Sexism is the same warped way of thinking and feeling about women. And the fact that many women have accepted sexist stereotypes for themselves and are even willing to rally around St. Phyllis to defend them, does not make a bit of difference. There have been, there still are, many Blacks who accept our stereotypes of them. Blacks who have it good as second-class persons, Blacks who defend the "place" which our "master race" has assigned to them. They are known as Uncle Toms. . . .

When it comes to being treated as less than persons, women have been put down just as much as Blacks have, though less crudely, of course. In fact, chivalry has been one of the softest, deadliest weapons for keeping women in their place. "I like to be helped into my overcoat," said a young woman. She did not realize she was about to make history until she added, "but not if it costs me $3,000.00 a year in salary." She might have added: "Nor if it confirms the stereotype about my being submissive rather than aggressive, emotional rather than rational, weak rather than strong, dumb rather than smart—all in the name of my precious femininity!"

THE BIBLE AND WOMEN

The struggle for women's rights comes home to us with particular vividness when we choose to listen to the debate as Christians.

There is no denying that the biblical writings are products of thoroughly patriarchal societies—the Hebrew first, then the Graeco-Roman. It is hardly surprising to find the man in the driver's seat, from Genesis through Revelation. What is surprising is that the overall male chauvinism is not consistent—that there are significant breakthroughs and advances toward a genuinely equal treatment of women not just in the New Testament but even in the Old.

For example, we keep bringing up the story of Adam's rib as proof of the natural or "original" inferiority of woman or of the awful sexism of the Bible—depending on where we are in our attitude and point of view. But that is only one Creation story! The other Creation story (Genesis 1:1–2:4) presents God as creating the first male and the first female at the same time, by the same divine act, equally in the "image of God"!

Again, while the Law of Moses would be judged sexist by twentieth-century standards, it gave women a much fairer deal than did any comparable code of law anywhere in the Ancient World. The Torah outlawed prostitution, protected adolescent girls, and provided for widows.

Sure, the work women did in ancient Israel was the age-old work of wives and mothers: drudgery. But even from their admittedly circumscribed position, some women managed to wield a great deal of power. Just read Proverbs 31:10–31, and you will marvel at the power which that "virtuous woman" wields over her household—including her husband!

Of course, the major breakthrough toward equal rights for women occurs in the New Testament, thanks to the spirit and the example of Jesus. Unlike other rabbis, Jesus always dealt with women as persons, whole persons with minds and souls of their own. He appreciated the religious conversation of Mary as much as He enjoyed the cooking of Martha, but He rebuked Martha for resenting Mary's spending time in study—a male preserve.

And there were, within the inner circle of his Disciples, women both named and unnamed who were to witness not only His crucifixion but also His Resurrection—women who thus became charter members of the Christian church.

Years later, the greatest of the Apostles would say about the Master: "In Christ, there is . . . neither male nor female," and he would be right, because that had been the Master's own life style, and that is how the Master would have it.

But wait. Is not this the same Paul, the whipping boy of Women's Lib? He certainly is, but quite unjustly so! Paul was actually far ahead of his time as regards the equal humanity of women, but there are indeed passages in the New Testament, a few by Paul, a few more ascribed to Paul, which prove that the New Testament, too, originated in a patriarchal world. We cannot get away from the fact that the biblical writings were written by men who were children of their time and culture. What we can do is to deal with the Bible intelligently, historically, testing everything in the Bible by the teachings and the spirit of Jesus. We can also rejoice in the fact that, as far as the status of women was concerned, so many of these writings were indeed ahead of their times—as if God were planting seeds of liberation in the soil of these societies, seeds which would one day bear freedom's fruit—when no human being would be treated as a faceless member of a group (be it a race or a sex), but every human being would be allowed to be a person, a beloved child of God made in His, or Her, Image. . . .

WE ALL NEED WOMEN'S LIB!

So let me pose the question again—and pose it straight this time: "Who needs Women's Lib?" And let me answer from deep and thoughtful conviction: we all do.

Yes, I believe that we all need to help finish the unfinished agenda of the women's rights movement. I also believe that all of us—not just women—but all of us stand to gain a great deal from the process of human liberation of which Women's Lib, the movement for the full and equal rights of women, is an essential part.

What women stand to gain is obvious: equal opportunity in the economy thanks to equal treatment under law; a greater number of socially accepted options for living; and the demolition of degrading stereotypes like "dumb blonde" or "castrating female" or "Jewish mother."

But men stand to gain a great deal, too. In a society where people are persons first and only incidentally male and female, men will gradually become less competitive, have fewer ulcers and untimely heart attacks. They will also be able to share the responsibility for making a living with their wives—without guilt or shame. Yes, in a society in which people can afford to be persons first, men will have a chance to be gentlemen, gentle men, without having gentleness mistaken for weakness.

It follows that children stand to gain a great deal from the ongoing liberation of women. Even now, in a growing number of families I know in San Francisco, both parents choose to work part time while the children are small, in order that the children may be raised by TWO PARENTS rather than by an inescapable mother and an occasional father. And these children are more likely to develop naturally, into normal manhood and womanhood, for having less pressure put upon them to grow "all boy" or "all girl," according to our polarized, ridiculously exaggerated notions of male-female roles!

Our country also needs Women's Lib. Population planning and control will be easier once the stigma, which still lingers, is removed from the single life: a stigma which continues to bear far more harshly on women than it does on men. After all, "bachelor" sounds like fun, but "spinster" or "old maid" suggests only wistfulness and frustration!

It is also plausible to believe that, if women constituted a majority in Congress, we would not be putting all our faith in weapons—and there would be fewer wars or, God willing, no more wars. We could have, and should have, gotten out of Vietnam years earlier, if we ever had to get into that tragic mess in the first place. But we could not endure losing face—a typical male chauvinist obsession!

Finally, speaking as a churchman, I am convinced that the church also stands to gain a great deal from the continuing liberation of women—the church with its badly checkered record in the treatment of women. It is already evident that the opening of traditionally male occupations in our churches, like the ministry, has begun vastly to enrich our spiritual life and vitality.

There is also a more subtle but, I believe, even more significant gain. The Gospel is about human liberation. Jesus Christ is God's unique gift to all who will receive Him—and the impact of His coming into your life or mine spells freedom: freedom from guilt, freedom from fear, freedom for life.

In the light of the Gospel, then, I find in Women's Lib, in the women's rights movement, two clear evangelical notes.

The first note is: DOWN with dominance/submission; up with caring/sharing.

The other note is: DOWN with stereotypes—like "men" or "women"; up with PERSONS, uniquely individual persons, gloriously different persons.

This is how Jesus saw people.

This is how Jesus dealt with people.

It is not too late for us to learn from Him! AMEN.

Comment: Who Needs Women's Lib?

I left Old First Church a little less than two years after this sermon. Under the next pastor, the church employed a staunchly feminist woman associate pastor who ministered effectively for a number of years. More and more employed women, both single and married, joined the church. Many of them who held executive positions during the week took on major projects in the church and are now among the congregation's most influential leaders. Of course these developments reflect societal changes, but I like to believe that "Who Needs Women's Lib?" helped prepare the way for them.

In addition to whatever this sermon might have contributed toward the empowerment of women in the congregation, I feel that it was useful, too, in giving me a chance once again to engage in a critical study of the Bible. You cannot get away from the fact that the world of the Bible was patriarchal in both Old Testament and New Testament times. What you can do is acknowledge the fact and then show how the teachings and spirit of Jesus pointed beyond patriarchy to the uniqueness and fundamental equality of all human beings.

A FAMILY CHURCH?

Context: A Family Church?

I left Old First Church, San Francisco, at the end of 1976, after seven years of service. I hoped to develop an itinerant ministry of preaching, adult Christian education and consulting with sessions and presbyteries, drawing on my eight years of experience as a professor of practical theology and on the broad range of contacts I had made during those years. It took me most of 1977 to prepare a menu of short courses, seminars, workshops from which pastors, presbytery executives, university chaplains and others could then order whatever struck them as relevant.

I do not regret the year and a half I spent "in the saddle," like an old-time circuit rider, covering the country from end to end in my 1963 VW "bug." I might have continued in this ministry indefinitely except for two drawbacks: I could not afford an agent or secretary, so I had to do all my own promoting, which I came to dislike very much; and the good income which I earned while on tour (6–8 weeks) did not make up for the lack of income during the 3 or 4 months I had to spend selling and setting up my next tour.

The invitation of the First Presbyterian Church of Vancouver, Washington, to the position of interim pastor came in the nick of time. I was glad to settle down again, for a while. I could not guess that the next 15 years of my life would be spent largely in interim pastorates: five in California, five in other states.

Vancouver, Washington at the mouth of the Columbia River is really a suburb of Portland, Oregon, though Vancouverites resent this description. The First Presbyterian Church, with about one thousand members at the time, felt and acted like a suburban church. It was all-white and consisted of all nuclear families, with only a number of elderly widows to remind one that there were also singles in the world.

It was quite a change from the exciting diversity of Old First Church's membership. It brought back to mind Gibson Winter's disturbing analysis of *The Suburban Captivity of the Churches,* which seemed as valid as when the book was first published in 1961.

"A Family Church?" takes issue with the assumption that the nuclear family, "father, mother and 2.2 children," is God's model for the Christian life. Noting the crisis of the American family, which was evident even then, I tried to show that God deals with persons and does not have any special stake in the family, let alone the American nuclear family.

A FAMILY CHURCH?

By John R. Bodo
Interim Pastor
First Presbyterian Church
Vancouver, Washington
July 29, 1979

SCRIPTURE: LEVITICUS 19:9–10, 13–14, 17–19
MATTHEW 5:43–48
MATTHEW 12:46–50

On this Mother's Day or Christian Home Sunday, I would like to reflect with you on the connection between the church and the family—the American nuclear family: father, mother, and 2.2 children.

A few weeks ago, I was driving past a neat, suburban church. Even without stopping, I had time to read the bulletin board which featured, of course, the name of the church and the name of the pastor. But then, in letters just as large, there were the words: *"A Family Church."*

My first reaction was: "That's nice. So what else is new?" The connection between church and family—defined as father, mother, and those 2.2 children— has been so close in American Protestantism that those three extra words, "A Family Church," might seem redundant. Like talking about a meal of food or a liquid drink.

But then I had some second thoughts on the subject, and it is those second thoughts that I would like to share with you. Question: is this equation between the church and the American nuclear family so natural, so right, as to be beyond critical reflection? Or is it perhaps time to entertain some second thoughts about defining the church as an extension of the nuclear family?

MIXED REPORT ON THE FAMILY

The first thing that needs to be said is that any survey of the American family today is bound to produce a mixed report.

There is no denying the traditional and continuing importance of the family. It is the basic unit of our society. When a man and a woman marry, their legal status changes along with their social and spiritual condition. And with the birth of their first child, further changes occur in their legal, social, and spiritual responsibilities and opportunities, whose significance can hardly be overrated. Yes, the American family continues to function as a basic economic and social unit as well as the primary laboratory for emotional and spiritual growth.

But the American family is also an endangered species. Any business with the failure rate of marriage in our country would not survive as a business. People simply would not get into a business with a failure rate of one in three, let alone one in two!

The sweeping changes in our society which are altering such basic institutions as marriage and the family have been causing Christians a great deal of bafflement and anxiety. The mixed report which the American family is earning in our times makes us feel nervous, depressed, wistful.

This wistfulness accounts for the lasting success of Thornton Wilder's nostalgic *Our Town,* and for the more recent crowning of that technicolor wallow in nostalgia, *On Golden Pond.*

Even the disquieting success of the so-called Moral Majority and the striking growth of the Mormon Church, especially in California, are directly related to our nervousness about families that do not pray together, seldom play together, and often do not stay together. Or even get together, since the percentage of single persons in our society has been growing by leaps and bounds.

THE BIBLE AND THE FAMILY

It may seem to us, then, that we are in a very bad way because the nuclear family—father, mother, and those 2.2 children—has come upon hard times in our society; and, if we believe that the nuclear family is the pattern God has designed for us, that it is the pattern for the good life, our feeling of depression is understandable.

But where did we get the idea that the nuclear family bears God's own stamp—that it is indeed God's own model for the Christian life?

"In the Bible," you might say. "Where else?"

Well let's see. . . .

In the Old Testament, the family is certainly taken for granted. Its significance is stated from the beginning, literally: the ancient myth of Eden is about a nuclear family—Adam and Eve and Cain and Abel, and, as an afterthought, the obscure Seth. Similarly, Hebrew history begins with God's choice of a married man, Abraham, who, within God's covenant is designated—along with his wife Sarah—as the original Patriarch of all the subsequent generations of the Chosen People.

We also find in the Old Testament a large number of early laws: establishing the absolute authority of father, assuring respect for mother, regulating inheritance rights, calling for justice for neighbors and generosity toward strangers. But the family as an institution is far from fixed. It is rather in a state of flux. There is gradual evolution from polygamy and concubinage toward monogamy, with recurrent alarm about intermarriage with Gentiles.

And within this evolving life of the Jews and of the Jewish family, there is a rich, motley cast of characters: good, bad, and mostly in-between. There are super-generous husbands like Hosea and severely straying husbands like David. There are model wives and mothers, like that of "Goody Two Shoes" Mother's Day Queen in Proverbs 31, and there are ghastly ones like Jezebel. There are faithful, though slightly dull sons like Esau, and crafty, self-seeking sons like Jacob, or Absalom.

Yes, the family is taken for granted in the Old Testament as the basic unit of society, sanctioned by the Creator. But nowhere is it suggested that family life represents God's unchanging will for personal obedience and social and spiritual fulfillment. On the contrary, God deals with persons—wherever they fit or do not fit into the changing family. Even from the dim beginnings of the race, God is a God of persons—the "God of Abraham, Isaac, and Jacob" who are not just symbols of the tribe or nation but also individuals, individually loved by God and individually accountable to Him.

The story is much the same in the New Testament, except for the fact that monogamy has carried the day, at least officially. Marriage and the family are still primarily socio-economic arrangements, endowed with religious sanctions for their protection, but never romanticized—or even theologized beyond a very earthy, practical level.

The earliest New Testament writings (for example, Paul's letters to the Church at Corinth) are decisively colored by the Early Church's belief that the end of the world and the return of the Lord lay just around the corner. As a result of this belief, Paul does not even recommend marriage, except as a vehicle for channeling and controlling sexual passion. Paul sets forth the single life as the preferred option because it offers fewer distractions and is more likely to assure "undivided attention to the Lord" (I Corinthians 7:35).

In Paul's later writings, for example, Colossians, and in the anonymous but strongly Pauline Letter to the Ephesians, belief in the imminent return of the Lord has faded and, as a result, a more positive view of marriage and family life appears. The relevant portions of Colossians 3 and Ephesians 5 are indeed remarkable for tempering father's absolute power, stressing mutuality of obligation and affection in marriage, and even making a nod toward the rights of children. But again, there is no suggestion that the family, let alone the nuclear family, is God's model for the Christian life.

JESUS AND THE FAMILY

But what about Jesus, then? Did not Jesus establish the family as special to God, deserving of all the Mother's Days, Father's Days, and Children's Days we have been adding to our secular/sacred calendars? Did He not, both by His teachings and by His example, point to the family as God's own pattern for the social and spiritual fulfillment of His children and the touchstone of their obedience to Him?

Well, one step at a time. First, what did Jesus teach about marriage and the family? To respond in just two words: nothing new. In fact, He said very little on the subject, which leads us to conclude that He was a loyal son of the Torah, in basic agreement with its teachings. But on those few points where Jesus did have something to say about marriage and the family, He made it crystal clear that—just like the Sabbath—marriage and the family exist for persons, at the service of individual human beings, rather than the other way around!

For example, Jesus accepted monogamy as the standard, and condemned adultery, but He interceded—at the risk of His reputation or life—to save a person guilty of adultery. Or again, Jesus rejected divorce except for adultery, but lashed out against the Law which chained a woman to her husband while making it possible for him to divorce her at a mere whim. Once more, Jesus' concern is for justice and compassion for persons. He offers no wholesale endorsement for any institution.

Nor can we make too much of Jesus' speaking of God as Father. The image which this word, Father, would conjure up in the minds of His hearers would be absolute power and only secondarily justice and mercy. Jesus' image of God as Father is clearly not drawn from the American nuclear family.

Well then, what about Jesus' example? Did He not come from a model home? Was He not a loving son of His mother and (earthly father) a caring brother for his three brothers and (at least) two sisters? And did He not say, "Let the little children come to me . . .? Yes, but . . . we project so much of our own American, Protestant, middle-class belief in the nuclear family into a few selected New Testament texts that the result is not exegesis, laying the truth of the text bare, but eisegesis, reading into the text what we want it to say. At the same time, we ignore other, quite explicit texts which call into question what we so much want to believe.

For example, everything we claim about the birth and youth of Jesus is either myth (like the Christmas stories) or speculation. The only story which tells about Jesus as a boy (Luke 2:41–52) shows Him already distancing Himself from Joseph and Mary, putting family loyalty—and even filial obedience—in its place: below one's primary responsibility to God. The incident foreshadows Jesus' saying about God and Caesar. Just like the nation, the family is entitled only to a limited loyalty.

Then, as soon as Jesus begins His ministry, His family, in effect, wash their hands of Him, while He sharply dissociates Himself from them and "adopts" His Disciples as His family. "Who is my mother? Who are my brothers? . . . Here are my mother and my brothers!"

Nor is this statement His strongest. Listen to Matthew 10, starting at verse 34:

> Do not think that I have come to bring peace on earth; I have come to bring not peace but a sword! For I have come to set a man against his father, and a daughter against her mother . . . and a man's foes shall be those of his own household. He who loves father or mother more than me is not worthy of me; and he who loves son or daughter more than me is not worthy of me. . . .

A GOD OF PERSONS—WITH OR WITHOUT FAMILIES

What does it mean, then, that we cannot make a case for the nuclear family, our kind of family, as God's model for human life, let alone for the Christian life? What does it mean that Jesus Himself makes no such case?

It means, negatively, that the family—like all human institutions—is an everchanging socio-economic institution in which God has no stake as such. The Gospel is not married to marriage, neither is it threatened by the rise in the divorce rate or the growing percentage of people who prefer the single life. Christianity can accommodate itself to other arrangements beside monogamous marriage and to alternative provisions for raising children responsibly and lovingly, just as the Christian church can operate and flourish under a variety of socio-economic systems rather than only under capitalism.

But there is also a positive answer to the question. God's concept of the family is different. Indeed, if we examine the Bible's use of family language with an open mind, we shall discover that family language in the Bible applies primarily to the human race and to the people of God, that is, first the Jews as a nation, then the world-wide Church of Jesus Christ.

It is to these two "families," and only to these two, that God has bound Himself in solemn covenant. Adam and Eve, "Mr. Man" and "Mrs. Life," are symbols of the human race. Abraham, Isaac, and Jacob, while individually portrayed, are symbols of their people, so that the stories about their family fortunes are actually stories about God's dealing with His people, Israel. And in the New Testament, God's New Covenant, the Church of Jesus Christ—composed of persons from all nations, all walks of life, single and married—becomes God's special family, set in the midst of His global family—to witness to His love for persons: persons first and last!

Yes, since Jesus Christ, God no longer has any stake in any nation as a nation, nor has God ever had any stake in your family or in my family. God loves us as persons: you as a person; your husband or wife as a person; your children as persons, and your parents, your telephone operator, and your trashman as persons. And God is deeply concerned that we do not use the alleged sanctity of the family as a pretext for oppressing and exploiting one another.

So, on this Mother's Day or Christian Home Sunday, let us by all means honor our mothers, respect our fathers, love our children; but let us avoid making a little tin god of "the family." Rather, let us remember the words of our Lord: "If you love (only) those who love you, what reward have you . . .?

The love which God expects of you and me includes your family and my family, but it begins with loving God's two families: the human race, especially the poor, the oppressed, the unlovely; and the worldwide Church of our Lord Jesus Christ. Amen.

Comment: A Family Church?

Several young and middle-young couples in the church heard this sermon as an attack on their Christian life style rather than as a plea for openness to self-criticism and to diversity. At a meeting of the couples' club just a few days later, we were able to clarify what I had or had not said and to smoke a peace pipe.

Today, twenty years later, the issue is more alive than ever. The conflict over "family values" is nationwide. Restoration of the *patriarchal* nuclear family is a major objective of the Christian Coalition and of such diverse, kindred organizations as the Promise Keepers and Louis Farrakhan's Million Men March. While the decline of the family is certainly a telling *symptom* of the sickness of our society, it is hardly its *cause.* But denouncing the decline offers a way to express homophobia and antifeminism in acceptable language.

The Presbyterian Church itself has moved sharply to the right on this front. Amendment B, approved by a majority of the presbyteries and (to be) adopted as a part of church law by the 1997 General Assembly, restricts ordination to the offices of minister, elder, and deacon to persons living either in chastity or fidelity within a man-woman marriage. "A Family Church?" may still be preached, but the *formal* commitment of the Presbyterian Church is to the nuclear family as God's model for the *full* Christian life. Note, though, that Amendment B passed by a very slim margin. Stay tuned!

MR. RICH MEETS LAZARUS

Context: Mr. Rich Meets Lazarus

My second interim pastorate was at the Westminster Presbyterian Church of Des Moines. The church claimed 2,800 members: the largest church I would ever pastor, even if you take off about 600 who were just "names on the roll." It was also the biggest Presbyterian Church in Iowa and the bellweather church in the Presbytery of Des Moines.

The occasion for "Mr. Rich Meets Lazarus" was the forthcoming annual special offering for the One Great Hour of Sharing. Received in most of the major Protestant communions since the end of World War II and providing most of the funds for the operation of Church World Service, the ecumenical worldwide relief agency of the National Council of Churches, OGH had been meeting with a good response in Westminster Church. There seemed to be no reason why the substantial receipts of 1979 could not be matched or exceeded at Pentecost, 1980.

Perhaps I should have let well enough alone, but since the congregation was prepared to hear about human need, I decided to approach the subject differently. This church, I realized, like most of our churches, could be generous in helping the poor, the victims of natural or man-made distress, as long as they could be kept at a safe distance. Thus the ratio of giving to "mission" (including OGH) to giving to the local church programs, though still modest, was fairly high. But the church gave far less to organizations trying to minister to human need in Iowa's capital, locally; and, so far as I recall, offered few if any opportunities to its members for dealing face to face with their "less fortunate" brothers and sisters.

In the sermon, which could not help being an indictment of "Mr. Rich," I was careful to include myself. I had long since learned that you do not get very far with people by just making them feel guilty. But I was being sincere; my discomfort in the presence of poor people, my passing up the opportunity to try out being poor in San Francisco for 48 hours, my failure to expose the pitfalls of the work ethic indicted me as much as they indicted anyone in the congregation or the congregation itself.

MR. RICH MEETS LAZARUS

By John R. Bodo
Interim Pastor
Westminster Presbyterian Church
Des Moines, Iowa
May 18, 1980

SCRIPTURE: LUKE 16:19–31

We do not know the name of the rich man in Jesus' parable. In the *Vulgate,* the Latin Bible, he is called Dives (Dee-ves), but that is simply a Latin word for "rich." So we might as well call him Mr. Rich.

Mr. Rich went to business every morning, passing the beggar, Lazarus, on his right. Mr. Rich came home every evening, passing Lazarus on his left. But Mr. Rich never really saw Lazarus.

Lazarus sat at Mr. Rich's door day in and day out. He had positioned himself strategically, right where the garbage came flying out. For Mr. Rich's garbage was the beggar's lifeline. If Mr. Rich had installed a garbage disposal, Lazarus would have starved.

The garbage kept coming. Lazarus stayed alive until he died. But Mr. Rich never saw him, never really saw Lazarus as a man, like himself. Face to face with Lazarus at least twice a day without ever seeing him, Mr. Rich could hardly be expected to recognize Lazarus in the world to come. But he did. . . . and the recognition came as a shock to Mr. Rich. . . .

FEELINGS ABOUT THE POOR

I do not really identify with Mr. Rich. Do you? Who does? Mr. Rich is a caricature of self-preoccupied callousness. I do not see myself that way at all. But right now, after doing some homework on the facts about world hunger, I am haunted by the notion that the world's poor—and that means every third or fourth person in the world—may be seeing me as Mr. Rich!

This haunting has compelled me to examine my own feelings about the poor, since hunger and poverty are inseparable. I hope to continue this self-examination for a long time, but I can tell you already that I do not like what I have begun to find out about my feelings.

Dominant by far among my feelings about the poor is discomfort. Face to face with a poor person, I simply don't feel at ease. There is the shabby clothing, the odor of poverty, the mixture of deference and hostility, the misuse of the King's English, the potential violence. I remember that years ago I had a chance to "play poor" for a couple of days, just to find out what it was like, and that I politely turned down the opportunity.

It was one of those Urban Training Institutes for the clergy. You reported to the downtown YMCA on Friday afternoon in your shabbiest clothes.

After an instruction session, you were let go, with four dollars in your pocket, for forty-eight hours. You were not permitted to contact anyone you knew. On four dollars you had to survive in San Francisco for two days and two nights, as thousands of people were doing, are doing, all the time. Then, on Sunday afternoon, what was left of you was allowed to return to the "Y" for a shower, a hot meal, and the sharing of experiences.

I didn't go—because I was scared—just as I would be to this day. But not going made me feel guilty, which brings me to my second strongest feeling about the poor: guilt. In my San Francisco church, we kept a food closet to which members brought canned goods or donated cash. Often I myself would drive to The Dented Can, in the Tenderloin, to replenish our stock. Our policy was that anyone who asked for help and would accept a bag of cans (and a can opener) would get one. Many declined, some in unprintable language. They wanted money. I didn't feel guilty about them. I did not consider it my moral responsibility to keep any man or woman in drink or drugs. But those who accepted the food made me feel guilty by their very existence, and also because I realized how little we were doing for them and how impersonally.

For underlying my discomfort and my guilt there has been helplessness. I really have not known what to do about poverty and hunger. In our great cities, poverty is concentrated in neighborhoods which you can tour from the safety of your car, though you would be foolish to stop. Rural poverty, however, is just as bad, often worse, except that it is scattered and hidden from view. And this in the United States, the richest country in the world! What about Asia, or Africa, or Latin America? I have been reading and reading. The statistics are overwhelming. I feel that I cannot keep up with them. I suspect that I really resist remembering them. And that, too, is part of my discomfort, my guilt, my helplessness. That, too, is where I have been with respect to poverty and hunger.

SPECIAL HANG-UPS OF CHRISTIANS

While becoming freshly conscious of my feelings about the poor, I have also become aware, newly aware, of certain hang-ups which I believe we all share as Christians, specifically as American Protestant Christians.

Hang-up No. 1 is our traditional commitment to charity. We may no longer use the word, but our instinctive response to the presence of poverty and hunger has not changed. We make a gift and turn away.

Mr. Rich in Jesus' parable is indeed a caricature. He would be far more believable if he were portrayed dropping a copper coin in Lazarus' grimy hat every day, or at least twice a week; and a silver coin, or even a gold coin, on high holy days. Mr. Rich would also be a liberal contributor to organized charity, both through his business and from his own pocketbook. And he would nod his approval of Jesus' words, "The poor you always have with you": though Jesus hardly meant those words for Mr. Rich's comfort!

Yes, as Christians we have been uncritically wedded to the practice of charity which does more for the giver than for the recipient—charity which offers minor, temporary relief to the hungry while making us feel full of virtue—charity which leaves the causes of poverty and hunger untouched.

Hang-up No. 2 is our judgmental attitude toward the poor grounded in the "Puritan ethic" which, in turn, is based on a self-servingly selective reading of the Bible. We are, most of us, quite unlike Mr. Rich. We are not business tycoons. We have worked hard all our lives. We are making it; a few of us very comfortably, most of us adequately. We have never been on welfare, nor accepted nor needed anyone's charity. So we tend to believe that the poor, whether in Appalachia, or Northern Brazil, or the slums of our great cities, are poor because they are not trying hard enough. If they were, would they not be making it, at least modestly, as we are?

St. Paul was understandably hostile toward willful idlers. He warned the Christians at Thessalonica that if a man refused to work, he should not expect to eat. That single statement, taken out of context, has worked like a miracle drug for uneasy Christian consciences! At the same time, we conveniently ignore the majority report in the Bible. We ignore the "poor laws" in Deuteronomy, which are the historic Magna Carta of welfare rights. We ignore the forceful pleading of Amos and Isaiah on behalf of the poor and the hungry, and their indictment of the hollow "tokenism" of charity. We ignore Jesus' own constant siding with the poor and His insistent warning of the rich.

So we continue to worry about "welfare chiselers"— whose mischief costs pennies compared to the cost of white collar crime or useless nuclear weapons. We are mesmerized by all the propaganda directed against the poor, because that is what we really want to believe, even though we know that the overwhelming majority of welfare recipients are children who did not ask to be born but are here now, and elderly people, many of whom would just as soon be dead, if only we let them die in peace with dignity. And we have been acquiescing with only minor resistance in the ongoing massacre of social assistance programs while accepting, in helpless indignation the additional billions thrown at the Pentagon. And all this, I repeat, because as devotees of the Puritan Ethic, we really have it in for the poor!

The third hang-up is closely tied to the first two: we refuse to admit that poverty and hunger are political.

As American Christians, we rightly cherish the separation of church and state. Unfortunately, we have perverted this doctrine into a virtual abdication of political responsibility. We do not deny that, as Christians, we are morally responsible for the relief of poverty and hunger. As Americans, we know that the richest and most powerful country in the world is in the strongest position to do something about world hunger and poverty. But our ignorance of politics is so profound that we refuse to see the next step, which is that only by political action can the government be persuaded to rearrange our national priorities, so that bread and justice for all will move up to first place, while greed, waste, and war are properly curbed.

As tentative as my conclusions are about the problem of hunger, I have arrived at one rock-firm conviction. It is this: the most immoral thing, the most cruel thing about hunger is that it is totally unnecessary. There is enough food around to feed the world's four billion people today. With new sources of food and constantly improving technologies, there will always be enough food to go around, provided we exercise reasonable population control. Hunger has become unnecessary and unjustifiable. The problem is political. It has to do with national priorities, with the arms race, with imperalism, with exploitation: problems whose solutions await political organization and political action.

Throughout my ministry, I have always worked hard to promote church-sponsored hunger relief charities like the Presbyterian Hunger Fund, or the annual ecumenical "One Great Hour of Sharing." I believe strongly in these programs. They do a great deal of good with an extremely low overhead. They deserve our generous response—and they will always be needed, just as there will always be a need for Bandaids.

But if our response, as Christians, to the twin plagues of hunger and poverty is only of the Bandaid variety, we are not being morally serious. We are playing games and salving our consciences. We are not really coming to grips with the problem, because the problem is systemic.

There is something wrong with the system which lets Mr. Rich live in luxury while Lazarus squats at his door, abjectly dependent on Mr. Rich's garbage. There is something wrong with the system, which allows six percent of the world's people, the Unites States, to consume forty percent of the world's goods. There is something wrong with the system which skimps on food stamps while hoarding 50,000 nuclear weapons.

I was proud of this church's response to the "One Great Hour of Sharing" appeal last spring. I hope that this year's response will be greater still. But I would urge you with equal urgency to acquaint yourselves with the politics of hunger and poverty—and to move beyond the practice of charity to the pursuit of bread and justice for all. . . . AMEN.

Comment: Mr. Rich Meets Lazarus

The offering for the One Great Hour of Sharing was duly received three weeks later and it did exceed the previous year's offering, but not spectacularly. At least the sermon did not, by its critical stance, undermine people's willingness to write another check.

But the sermon also had a positive, though indirect, effect. By pointing out that "poverty and hunger are political," that the president, or the governor, or even the mayor can, by one stroke of the pen, do more good or harm to the poor than all the churches combined, I raised the consciousness of three elders who took the initiative to lobby Session into organizing a Church and Society Committee. This committee began to let the membership know, through the church newsletter, about opportunities for individual political action in Congress, in the State Legislature, in the City Council. Instead of only writing checks to help victims of the system, members were now being schooled in ways to change the system in favor of the victims, by writing or phoning legislators when some action was pending or needed.

Right now, 17 years later, we have a new welfare law which is largely an "end welfare" law. The churches cannot replace or even mend the safety net which is being shredded. They can and will continue to provide both money (e.g., through OGH) and volunteers to help the poor. But the churches can help, through their members, to recall the government to its responsibility for a strong safety net. What the Christian Right has helped dismantle, the Christian Center and Left can help to restore.

PILGRIMAGE WITH DETOURS

Context: Pilgrimage with Detours

San Marino, a bedroom suburb of Los Angeles, had 14,000 inhabitants in 1981 but not a single rental unit. There was no home under $250,000 in the community. The manse (parsonage), which I would inhabit by myself except when Mary would fly down for a visit, was a $500,000, five-bedroom, four-bath wonder. San Marino also had a gorgeous park and sports center which closed on weekends, lest residents from the surrounding Hispanic communities invade and pollute it. The characteristics of the membership of the church can readily be inferred from the foregoing information.

The Community Presbyterian Church of San Marino was bitterly divided over a recent scandal in which the pastor, since disciplined and dismissed by the presbytery, had been found guilty of multiple adultery. So serious was the discord that presbytery in effect took over the governance of the congregation. Thus I was not elected by the membership as interim pastor but imposed on them by the presbytery as Stated Supply, an old Scottish term no one knew or liked!

Being perceived as presbytery's henchman, I knew that I had to win the people's trust, somehow, and that I would also have to distract them from their infighting over their fallen idol by creating interest in and, most likely, conflict over some substantial issue or issues. Thus I decided to preach a frankly "first person" sermon, mixing autobiography with opposition to the nuclear arms race which, I hoped, would lead to churchwide study of the issue as well as participation in the Presbyterian church's controversial Peacemaking Program.

I had obtained permission from the Session to solicit a special "peacemaking offering" on Worldwide Communion Sunday (October 4), the date targeted by the denomination. I had also been authorized by the session to design a six-week seminar for adults on the Cold War, starting on the same date.

I needed a connecting link between my hope to win the congregation's trust and my resolve to interpret and promote the denomination's Peacemaking Program. The link turned out to be "Presbyterian." On this point, I was to find out, there would be at least as much resistance as there would be to anyone's questioning the premises and conduct of the Cold War! For the San Marino church was hardly Presbyterian at all, showing little interest in or loyalty to the denomination. That was why they resented my being thrust upon them by the presbytery. That was why they would have pocket-vetoed the infant Peacemaking Program. That was why they had chosen the corporate name, San Marino Community Presbyterian Church, a clear signal of where they stood.

The sermon fell into three predictable parts. (1) "Pilgrim": a capsule spiritual autobiography, based on Jesus' words to the Twelve (John 15:12–17), especially on the reminder, "You have not chosen me, but I have chosen you. . . ." (2) "Presbyterian": related to Isaiah 55:6–11, a tribute to the Presbyterian Church in terms of my personal debt to the church; and (3) "Peacemaker": an indictment of the suicidal folly of the nuclear arms race, based on Romans 12:14–21, and inviting the congregation's participation in the Presbyterian Peacemaking Program. I still remember vividly that I had to cut my original draft to less than half its length!

PILGRIMAGE WITH DETOURS

By John R.Bodo
Interim Pastor
Community Presbyterian Church
San Marino, California
September 27, 1981

OLD TESTAMENT: ISAIAH 55:6–11
EPISTLE: ROMANS 12:14–21
GOSPEL: JOHN 15:12–17

This is not going to be a sermon in the strict sense. It is going to be an epistle—from me to you. Among Christians, an epistle should be as acceptable as a sermon. Paul, at least, would approve.

I have been with you for four months, but many of you don't know me yet. I don't even mean those who do not come to church. I am talking about you, many of you, who are here every Sunday.

Appearing at this formidable height in this formal robe may lend distance but not necessarily enchantment. I am not trying to enchant you—or anyone. I am trying to be myself, and to do the work to which I have been called. But I am aware of the distance, the needless distance. I deplore it. And I am seeking your help to overcome it.

Recently, I took part with the Session in two in-house retreats on the informal theme, "Where are you coming from, John Bodo?" I was a bit nervous about the question, because I knew that "Budapest" would not be considered a sufficient answer! But both retreats turned out deeply rewarding to me. I believe that they were helpful to all participants. It came out, for example, that I would have had some initial obstacles to overcome no matter who I was, just because my name was not Rick. Two elders were gracious enough to admit that they had made up their minds they would not like me, but were unable to live up to their resolution. I was not looking for strokes, but I would not be human if I did not feel grateful to receive some!

Perhaps being human is what this is all about. Perhaps by becoming more human to you, across this unwanted distance, I might be able to reduce some of the strangeness, build some trust and, who knows? maybe even a little affection.

So let me try, please, to share with you a bit more of my humanity by telling you a few things about myself in terms of three words, around which are wrapped my life's deepest loyalties.

PILGRIM

The first word is pilgrim. Conceived by Paul, popularized by *Pilgrim's Progress,* the image of the Christian as pilgrim speaks of journey, hardship, surprises, and constant change—with a promise, out of sight most of the time, at the far end of the road. The image also implies a call: God's call to take that first step—God's patient, persistent re-calls along the winding road.

Well, the detours on my pilgrimage, which eventually led me to become a Presbyterian minister, were rather spectacular. My parents and their families "converted" from Judaism at the end of World War I, when thousands of Jews were finding a haven of sorts in the Roman Catholic Church. Thus I was born and baptized a Roman Catholic.

As a little boy, however, I also suffered from severe asthma, until my parents were at their wits' end with me. Then, at the ripe age of seven, the priest who was instructing all the little Catholics in our school, waxed graphic about the fate of the damned in Hell—and I went home and had the worst attack of asthma of my life. I nearly died.

Now it so happened that we were living in a building owned by Budapest's only Unitarian congregation, whose offices were just above our apartment. In his indignation and anxiety, my father marched himself up to the Unitarian bishop's office, told him the whole story, and asked for admission to the fold, for the three of us. So there I was, an instant Unitarian; and you might know that, in Europe, Unitarians are really liberal Protestants—with baptism, the Lord's Supper, even bishops.

My first, dim inkling of a "call" came through the pastor who was preparing us for Confirmation. A thin, sallow, gently smiling young man, he was dying of tuberculosis while living entirely for others. His death, shortly after my Confirmation at age fourteen, made me think—and feel. I was a little bit hooked.

Meanwhile Hitler was rising over Europe. In Hungary, Hitler's reluctant ally, we might have felt safe, at least for a while. But my father was clairvoyant. While his friends thought that he was crazy, he enrolled us with the American Consulate for emigration. The same year, 1938, the year of Hitler's take-over of Austria, the year of the Anglo-French sell-out at Munich, I started my theological studies at the University of Geneva, Switzerland.

Did I feel any "call" during this next detour in my pilgrimage? No—and yes. I had agreed to study theology because it seemed the plausible thing to do and because I had no other commanding talents (except perhaps music). But I found little interest in the drily academic courses, and the saccharine, moralistic piety of my fellow-students and their families turned me off. But there was, once again, one man—August Lemaitre, Chairman of the Department of Theology. I am quite certain now that someone had planted him there, for me! Lemaitre introduced me to John Calvin's thought, to Calvin's grand intellectual sweep, to Calvin's insistence upon the relevance of the Gospel for society rather than just for individuals. I was now half-hooked.

We got out alive, all three of us, on one of the last passenger ships to leave from Lisbon for the United States. We arrived at Hoboken, New Jersey—what a ghastly way to fulfill one's dream of freedom!—on January 7,

1941, five days before some of you signed up to charter this church with the presbytery. So you became Presbyterians before I did, because I was still a Unitarian! I did not become a Presbyterian until a year or so later, thanks to three giants of the Reformed/Presbyterian family.

There was Henry Sloane Coffin, President of Union Seminary, New York, who welcomed me warmly and allowed me to continue my studies at once, even though I hardly knew how to ask for the time of day in English. There was Reinhold Niebuhr, a prophet of social justice in the tradition of Amos and Jesus who, more than anyone, kept me in the ministry by further expanding my consciousness of the intellectual and social relevance of the Gospel. And there was George Arthur Buttrick, pastor of the Madison Avenue Church, which we joined, and where I was ordained, on October 18, 1942, by the Presbytery of New York: the first twenty-two-year-old Hungarian-Jewish-nearly-American Presbyterian minister in the history of the world!

Talk about a pilgrimage with detours! No wonder that I love the words of our Lord addressed to His disciples and recorded in John 15: "You did not choose me, but I chose you . . .!" Few of us are called by the Lord as unmistakably as Paul was, who not only tore his pants when he fell off that horse but was also struck blind for a while— just to make sure that he got the message. Most of us can only trace our call in retrospect. For my part, after thirty-nine years in the ministry, I am quite certain that I was chosen; that my peculiar pilgrimage, with all its crazy detours, was guided by the strong, gentle hand of One Whose love gives lots of rope but will not let us go. . . .

PRESBYTERIAN

The second word which expresses a nearly lifelong and constantly growing love for me is Presbyterian. Some of you, I gather, believe that I have been "coming on too strong" as a Presbyterian. Let me tell you: you don't know how hard I have been holding back! When you love something as deeply as I love our church, it is not easy to be casual, to measure out your appreciation, your enthusiasm, with a teaspoon!

Remember: while God claimed me for a Christian, I chose to become a Presbyterian. There were other options, but I made my choice, and I have never regretted it! But if you think that I came to this church as presbytery's henchman—to put something over on you, to fit you into some pre-fab mold, please think again! I love the Presbyterian Church! I came to it as an adult, by a long and winding road. During the next twenty-nine years, I was confirmed in the rightness of my choice! That is why I seem to be "coming on strong . . .!"

Let me try to account to you for my deep commitment to our Presbyterian system of faith and practice by using my father's favorite biblical passage, Isaiah 55.

There are two statements in Isaiah 55, which are made to order for Presbyterians. We read first: "For my thoughts are not your thoughts, neither are my ways your ways, says the Lord." As a Presbyterian, I find in these words a resonant affirmation of our emphasis on God's sovereignty, God's majesty, God's Hebrew Fatherhood, which puts to shame all notions of God as "Daddy." As Presbyterians, we expect God to be God. We also expect to trust Him, even though we cannot understand His ways, and to keep loving Him, even when He seems to be crushing us—with calamity or with silence.

The other statement in Isaiah 55 follows immediately: "For as the rain and the snow come down from Heaven and return not thither but water the Earth, giving seed to the sower and bread to the eater, so shall my word be that goes forth from my mouth: it shall not return to me empty, but it shall accomplish that which I purpose. . . ." It is the circular motion, the wholeness, contained in this image which enthralls me. It is a gloriously Presbyterian image of God's action in the world.

The Presbyterian system of faith and practice is one of motion and wholeness. No "word" from God is ever the last word. God remains as involved with us as water: sometimes as rain falling, sometimes as moisture evaporating to form fresh clouds, for the next rain. It is God who compels change and God whose faithfulness provides continuity.

Let me illustrate my point first, with our Presbyterian theology. We are a confessional church. We believe in working out, carefully, the framework of our faith. But our present confession is called the *Confession of 1967* which announces, by its very title, that it is not meant to be the last word, that there will be need, surely for a *Confession of 2017*, or whatever. There is wholeness of faith for you, with built-in room for motion, for change!

Let me illustrate, next, with our Presbyterian polity—the structure and process with which we govern ourselves. We are a connectional church. The life of the church flows from the congregations up through the presbyteries and synods to the General Assembly, and from the General Assembly down once more, in a steady, circular motion which almost literally resembles the metaphor of rain and cloud. The system is a model of wholeness, in which Paul's image of the body and its members is a palpable reality, and "decently and in order" is a passionate commitment.

Let me illustrate, once more, with our Presbyterian social conscience. John Calvin felt that God was claiming the whole city of Geneva for righteousness, not just the Christian minority. John Knox felt the same way about the realm of Scotland, just as Amos and Jeremiah had felt about their nation. In the Presbyterian curriculum of discipleship, concern for the public life—for justice, peace, freedom—has always been a required course, not a take-it-or-leave-it elective! The Presbyterian system knows only one gospel, personal and social. There is wholeness and there is constant motion. Yesterday's understanding of freedom, peace, justice may no longer be adequate today. Change is taken for granted, because God is the Lord of history. . . .

I love the Presbyterian Church. I am constantly challenged by its theology, disciplined by its polity, prodded by its social conscience. I beg you therefore: give me a chance to help you get to know the church better! Give me a chance to share more of this great love of my life with you while I am around: in the course on "Our Heritage and Our Mission" which I will be starting soon; in warmly welcoming my beloved friend, Jan Willette; in our Officer Training Program; and in participating with me in the life of our presbytery, with its rich mix of Christians and its great needs, where a church like ours could be, should be, of so much help!

PEACEMAKER

Pilgrim—Presbyterian—the third is Peacemaker. There are today as many issues as ever, which engage the mind, the conscience, the faith of Christians. But, in a tragic sense, there is only one issue: one which overrides all the others by promising, or rather threatening, to "solve" all of them, once and for all, with finality. The issue is, of course, that impossible probability, nuclear war; and when I say nuclear war, I include those twin obscenities—chemical war and germ war.

Please remember: we started it all. We dropped the first A-Bomb, and the second, on two defenseless cities teeming with civilians. We showed the way to all other nations, including the Soviet Union, with whom we are now engaged in a spiraling, suicidal stalemate.

It did not have to happen this way. At the end of World War II, we spent billions of dollars on the Marshall Plan—to rebuild Germany and Japan, our enemies. Can you imagine how different things could have been if we had been only half as generous to our allies, the Russians? Russia was devastated: she had lost tens of millions of her people. What if we had reached out in friendship to her people who had stood between us and Hitler, who had done so much of our dying for us . . .?

Well, you may say, you can't undo thirty years of Cold War history! Can't you, really? What alternative is there? Every new weapon, every new system of weapons, increases the probability of ultimate disaster, intentional or accidental. In the name of security, we are buying insecurity. In the name of defense, we are preparing humankind for a global Jonestown!

I was not a pacifist as long as wars could, as a last resort, redress some intolerable wrong, like a Hitler. I am not a strict pacifist even now. As a Calvinist, my pessimism about human nature tells me that some kind of police force will always be necessary, within nations as well as under international auspices. But nuclear war? Today? Today's weapons are so unimaginably destructive that bombs like the ones we dropped on Hiroshima and Nagasaki were not even mentioned in the SALT talks; they were too puny to be worth mentioning!

So, along with Pilgrims and Presbyterians, I have been and am trying to be a Peacemaker. I worked hard, in the Fifties, to make peace—with justice—whether Blacks should have the same access to adequate housing as they already had to food or cars. We did not bring in the Kingdom, but we made a sizable dent in the ghetto walls of Princeton, New Jersey, and we helped prepare the way for the nation's first fair housing laws.

I also worked hard, in the Sixties, for dialogue, mutual listening and, hopefully, reconciliation, between people over thirty enmeshed, helplessly or willingly, in the Vietnam War, and people under thirty, on the Macalester College campus, who rejected the Vietnam War as morally wrong and refused to either kill or be killed in it. Again, we did not bring in the Kingdom, but our efforts helped a tiny bit toward speeding the end of the war.

But today I am deeply perplexed. It is not the threat of a nuclear holocaust; that I see all too clearly. What perplexes me is fellow-Christians, for whom peace seems to have become a dirty word!

What happened to Romans 12? "Bless those who persecute. . . . Repay no one evil for evil. . . . No, if your enemy hunger, feed him. . . . Do not be overcome by evil, but overcome evil with good. . . ." what happened to our faith?

By the monsters of technology we have unleashed and by our blind trust in them, we are one short step from the end of human life, certainly the end of all civilized life, on Earth. Is this what God created us for—with infinite care, patience, and love? Is this what He sent, sacrificed, and saved our Lord Jesus for? And must I acquiesce in this obscene, blasphemous scenario, not just for myself who has at least lived sixty-one years, but for Kawena, my grandson, age two . . .?

Tomorrow or the next day, you shall receive in the mail a letter from me, along with a response form and offering envelope. The letter will tell you about our church's program called Peacemaking—a churchwide, nationwide program of study and mission on behalf of peace. I am inviting you to respond in as many ways as God leads you. I am asking you, with the utmost urgency, to make a generous gift to the special Peacemaking Offering, which we shall receive next Sunday at our Worldwide Communion Services. Gathered around the Table of the Prince of Peace, with our gifts, we shall celebrate and pray for the oneness of His church, and of His world.

Beyond this request, I have a personal plea of just two words: trust me. Trust me, as I trust our Presbyterian Church, and as our church is daring us to trust the power of love over distrust and hate.

There are more detours ahead of me, I am sure, if God permits me to continue on my pilgrimage. But the great loves of my life—for our Lord Who called me and got me going on the road, for our Presbyterian Church, and for the cause of peace—are not likely to change. So use them. Use me. That is what I am here for. Amen.

Comment: Pilgrimage with Detours

While the majority remained at least slightly hostile or just unmoved, an important minority, especially of the Session, expressed appreciation for my sharing with them something about my background and major commitments. This turned out to be a significant lesson for me. I learned something about the potential of the "confessional mode" for getting beyond impasses between leaders and constituencies.

The Peacemaking Offering, received the following Sunday, was a mere token in terms of the church's size and financial strength, but its symbolic significance was considerable. Without "Pilgrimage with Detours," the offering would not have been authorized—or even mentioned.

Attendance at the peace study group turned out to be surprisingly large. I did not suspect to find as many Doves in the church. Few, however, of the vast majority of Hawks would expose themselves to any critique of our pursuit of the Cold War. The course did set an important precedent. Over against those who would argue that nothing "political" should ever be mentioned in church, it proclaimed, quietly but eloquently, that even the hottest issue could be and should be discussed by the congregation in biblical/theological perspective.

At the time I preached "Pilgrimage with Detours," the church was in tatters over their former pastor's spectacular indiscretions. Just nine months later, they were able to call a new pastor by a near-unanimous vote. It was a miracle only the Spirit of God could perform, but I sincerely believe that my ministry, and this sermon in particular, helped make it possible. After this sermon, I was no longer presbytery's henchman standing alone against 1,500 angry or sullen members. I had allies who would help me work for reconciliation within the congregation. A few of them I had even won over to a reconciling approach toward "The Enemy," the USSR. So if I had a chance to do it over, I definitely would. . . .

CHRISTIANS AND REVOLUTION

Context: Christians and Revolution

The nine months I spent as interim pastor of the First Presbyterian Church of Salt Lake City felt like a sojourn in a foreign country. We were still in the USA. American English was spoken. But the Mormon presence was so pervasive, the dominance of the Mormon church so complete, that we might as well have been journeying abroad. And this impression was daily confirmed by Presbyterians, members of First Church, who had been living in Utah for decades.

There was, in the church a "minority complex," a feeling of inferiority, of marginality shared by all the other mainstream Protestant churches and probably by the Catholics and the Evangelicals as well. But First Presbyterian Church was also suffering from severe "withdrawal symptoms" following the long pastorate of a capable and conscientious pastor, who was also a rigid soloist and benevolent tyrant. The fact that, on his retirement, he chose to stay in town would keep the church under his shadow even longer.

I could not attack, directly, either the Mormon Church or the lively ghost of the ex-pastor. Nor could I express, directly, my despair over Ronald Reagan and Reaganism. What I could do and tried to do was to initiate changes, at least in the church program, in order to remind people that change is possible and may even be desirable, not just in this "We've always done it this way" congregation, but perhaps even in Utah and in the United States. The changes I initiated were modest—like adopting a minimum standard for membership or broadening the church's leadership base—and the standpatters fought them every inch of the way.

"Christians and Revolution" was an outcry against the status quo, in our churches and in our country, in the name of the victims of the status quo. It struck me that all the "revolutions" which began in the Sixties, ground to a slow halt in the Seventies, and were now being buried under Reagan, had a common denominator. They were pleas or protests by persons "seeking their full human rights . . . over and against all impersonal data such as race, social class, education, age, sex. . . ."

This fundamental revolution, underlying all the particular revolutions (in race relations, in education, in sexual conduct, etc.), I considered—and still consider—unstoppable, even though 1983 showed a long backtrack from, say, 1968. Speaking to a congregation composed largely of "change resisters," I drew heavily on examples of the precedent-breaking, and sometimes law-breaking nonconformity of Jesus; and I closed by reminding those who might still be listening that "George Washington did not lead a conference or an excursion, but a revolution."

It was a broadside—and a gamble. But I believed that anyone who had been working with me (or against me) on specific changes in the church program would at least understand where I was "coming from."

CHRISTIANS AND REVOLUTION

By John R. Bodo
Interim Pastor
First Presbyterian Church
Salt Lake City, Utah
January 16, 1983

SCRIPTURE: ROMANS 12:1–2
GALATIANS 3:23–27
MATTHEW 11:28–30

A small town in South Dakota, or maybe it was in North Dakota, was celebrating its centennial. The accidental hero of the occasion was an old man whose date of birth coincided with the founding of the town. "Well, Sir," said a TV interviewer to the old man, "you must have seen quite a few changes in your 100 years in this town!" "I sure have, son," replied the old man, "I sure have, and I've opposed every one of them!"

This is how some Christians relate to change, but it is not necessarily the Christian way. Nevertheless, when change is rapid, indeed revolutionary, it is human to feel confused—and threatened. Members of the Moral Majority, or even the Ku Klux Klan, may be dangerous, but they are not devils with horns and club feet; they are mostly average Americans who feel confused and threatened by the revolution in which we are all caught up.

What revolution are we talking about? Are there not many, concurrent revolutions—racial, educational, sexual, and so forth? Yes and no. It is true that, for the last two decades, we have been witnessing revolutionary changes in these areas and in several others. But all these "single issue" revolutions really add up to one revolution, a revolution of rights. The fundamental issue underlying this revolution is persons—men, women and, yes, children, seeking their full human rights, from the basic right to stay alive under the shadow of nuclear annihilation to what I choose to call the right to be myself.

"I have a right to be myself!" is the cry. "I have a right to be myself over against all impersonal data—such as race, social class, education, age, sex" by means of which I have been classified, stereotyped, terrorized! Yes, this revolution—which has been slowed but not stopped—is about protecting, valuing, and helping people as persons, as unique individuals, beyond all labels.

BLACKS

Example: Blacks. For centuries, black people wore the label which our white forbears had pasted on them. They were different, therefore inferior, therefore ashamed to be black. That was the most tragic result of white racism: that Blacks actually accepted the label, believed it, lived down to it!

Then came "Black is Beautiful!" The white racist myth began to crumble not because everything or everyone black is actually beautiful, but because the slogan marked the beginning of black self-acceptance and cultural pride. No more hair straighteners! No more slavish copying of the Man's fashions! The black revolution raised the cry, "I want to be myself!" And that cry was picked up, on short order, by Native Americans, Asian-Americans, Hispanic-Americas. "I want to be myself! I want to be judged as a person rather than by my skin color or ethnic origin!"

THE POOR

Example: the poor. Until a little over a hundred years ago, a poor person who could not find work was reduced to begging. The condition of the poor had not really changed at all since Jesus' day. If anything, the Industrial Revolution had made things worse for the poor. Then, in the post-Civil War period, poor people began to seek strength in numbers, in organizing unions, and after another half-century of repression, both legal and violent, Congress enacted the country's first labor law, in 1936.

But to this day, masses of the poor are still not in unions. Nor does union membership work any miracles when there is no employment—and gadgets have continued, non-stop, to displace workers. So we have welfare, organized welfare, the contemporary equivalent of old-fashioned "charity."

Well and good, we have pretty much made our peace with the notion that, in the richest country in the world, nobody should literally starve—that some form of welfare should protect the life of those who otherwise would starve. But what about welfare rights? For the past decade or so, the poor have shown themselves increasingly reluctant to stand before the rest of us, hat in hand, begging for our bounty, and saying "Thank you, Sir!" and "Thank you, Ma'am!"—for any crumbs from our tables. Of course, they do not use slogans like "Poor is beautiful!", but the thrust is the same. The poor today expect to be accepted and assisted not out of "charity" but as a matter of right. "I have a right to live and to be myself, even if at the moment I am unable to produce anything with a price tag!"

SCHOOLS

Example: schools. Until recently, it was assumed that every child had to be educated in a mass situation and in much the same way, and that the primary function of education, or at least of public education, was to prepare children and young people to become productive units in the economy. Today, while the revolt against assembly-line schools has suffered some setbacks, it has also pretty much carried the day. We have come to take it for granted that educational systems must provide for what in the jargon is called "differentials in learning readiness." Special education across the full spectrum, from retarded to prodigy, is here to stay. In short, it has become an axiom that society bears some responsibility for the uniqueness of every child and young person, and that schools at all levels must acknowledge and incorporate this uniqueness. This, too, is a part of the revolution of rights—the revolution against all general, arbitrary, handicapping educational standards and practices.

AGE

Another example: age. This phase of the revolution of rights can be readily illustrated from both ends of the spectrum: youth and old age.

For youth, let us only recall the recent Constitutional Amendment lowering the voting age to 18. Some of us feared the worst. It did not happen. Eighteen-year olds as a group within the body politic, are acting as responsibly—or as irresponsibly—as their elders. They have proved beyond a doubt that they can be safely treated as individual human beings rather than as a group stereotype.

As for the elderly, it was not so long ago that they were supposed to retire and just fade away, like old soldiers. Who could foresee a national organization like the splendid Gray Panthers? But now "senior power" is a taken-for-granted fact of our economic and political life. People past sixty have begun to organize, to help themselves, to take pride in themselves. Why, indeed, should everyone retire at 65 when some people are alive and creative at 85, while others are duds at 45? Or 25? So once again the cry resounds, "I want to live and I want to be myself! I want to contribute and to be valued and helped as a person—never mind my ID card!"

SEX

One more example: sex. The so-called sexual revolution has certainly been the best advertised phase of the revolution of rights and, for many people, the most disturbing, because it has challenged some of our oldest superstitions and infiltrated some of our most carefully constructed defenses. The impact of the sexual revolution goes far beyond any change in sexual conduct, which may or not be as extensive as we may have been led to believe. The sexual revolution has affected all of our assumptions about what is male and what is female as well as about male-female roles in the economy and in society. Wherever people find themselves on the male-female spectrum, they are putting us all on notice with the same revolutionary cry: "I want to be myself! Straight or gay, single, married, or divorced: I have a right to be myself! And if I am different from what you expect me to be, that may just be your problem!"

CHRISTIANS AND THE REVOLUTION OF RIGHTS

What background and equipment do we, Christians, have for understanding and constructively dealing with this many-faceted revolution of rights?

The Gospel came into a world where persons were rigidly classified, stereotyped, labeled. Everyone had his place, like servants used to have their place; and, as as a rule, everyone was chained to his place, literally or figuratively, for life.

Ruling the scene was a master race, the Romans. The Romans had varying degrees of scorn for members of all other races. They could afford to be scornful: the Roman Empire was at the peak of its power, unchallenged, unconquerable.

But Jesus and the Apostles had a problem not only with the Romans but also with their fellow-Jews, because the Jews, too, were a master race of sorts at that time. The Jews believed themselves to be God's master race, as a nation; they labeled, and scorned all non-Jews as "goyim," "Gentiles," "other people."

Furthermore, whether in Rome or in Jerusalem, only men were persons. In Judaism, women were considered so obviously inferior that it required ten males to organize a synagogue and that no service of worship could be held unless ten males were present, even though there might be ninety women around. As for women under Roman law, they were chattel. Their place was the same Hitler would assign to them nineteen centuries later: *Kinder, Kirche, Kueche*—children, church, kitchen.

But even men were not all persons because the poor certainly did not count. Many of the poor, in turn, were sold into slavery. And everyone knew that a slave was not a human being at all, but a thing.

Against this backdrop, then, calling the Gospel revolutionary is not just appropriate: it is an understatement! Recall once again Paul's words to the Christians in the province of Galatia: "There is neither Gentile nor Jew, there is neither slave nor free, there is neither male nor female: for you are all one in Jesus Christ." If this is not a trumpet call to the original revolution of rights, I don't know what is!

And Paul did not compose that trumpet call. No, it was Jesus, Paul's Lord and ours, who composed it!

So, Jews had no dealings with Samaritans?

Jesus told a story in which two model Jews were the heavies while a Samaritan was the hero!

So, Jewish women were supposed to stay in their place?

Martha did: she stayed in the kitchen. But Jesus commended Mary for joining His seminar, and she was probably the first woman ever in a rabbi's class!

So, children were supposed to be seen but not heard?

Jesus set that little child at the center of the circle of the Disciples and told them that, in order to find out what the Kingdom of God was all about, they had to become like that little child!

So, sexual nonconformists were beyond the pale?

But Jesus saved the life of the woman patently guilty of adultery, made her accusers slink away in shamefaced confusion, and gave her a chance at a new, forgiven life.

So, the poor were supposed to beg, or at least to keep out of sight?

But Jesus pointed out how hard it would be for the rich to enter the Kingdom, and He singled out for special praise the poor widow's small gift—far above the lavish benefactions of the wealthy!

Yes, when Paul wrote, "Do not be conformed to the world, but be transformed by the renewing of your mind" (Romans 12–2), he was expressing, in unforgettable words the effect of the Gospel upon anyone who has really heard the Gospel.

How do we conform to the world? By accepting the labels which the world pastes on us, the place which the world assigns to us, the price tag which the world hangs on us!

And what happens to us when we are transformed by the hearing of the Gospel? We begin to accept ourselves as persons, as unique human beings created by a loving God, as individuals for whose sake God's only Son lives, suffers, dies and irresistibly rises, again and again, so that we may have life, life with self-respect, life abundant!

When we are, to use Paul's favorite phrase, *en Christo*, "in Christ"; when we discover, with Augustine, that God loves each of us as if there were only one of us; when, thanks to the Gospel, we are able to reject the false value which others have placed on us and to accept the amazing claim that, in God's sight, we are, each of us of infinite value—then we have indeed been transformed, revolutionized, the bloodless way— except for the blood of our Lord shed for all of us and for each of us, on the Cross!

So what is our responsibility with respect to the revolution of rights which, I repeat, goes on, irresistibly, despite obvious present setbacks? I have already given away my own answer by saying "irresistibly." I believe that this revolution is nothing other than the leaven of the Gospel stirring up new life in our time. It is a profoundly Christian revolution, even though some of its boldest fighters may not be Christian at all while some of its worst foes gargle with the Bible! Thus I believe that our responsibility is to help: to help every man, woman and child in the world attain the goal of that brave cry: "I want to live and to be myself!"

This grand cry for liberation calls for Christians to accept responsibilities appropriate to their condition. In El Salvador or in Poland, the primary responsibility of Christians is surely to do their share, along with non-Christians, in the struggle to remove the oppressor's heel. But those four American nuns, who went to El Salvador to teach the poor how to farm and how to read and were murdered by the Junta's goon squads financed and trained with our tax money, lay a different responsibility upon us who are living here, where dissent and protest are still possible. Our responsibility is voluntarily to take upon ourselves the yoke of the poor, the oppressed, the exploited, wherever they may be: in El Salvador, in Poland, or in our own country; to take their yoke upon ourselves, voluntarily, and to fight for their liberation—even if our own government is perpetuating, or decisively assisting in, their oppression.

For when Jesus, our Lord, offers us His yoke, it is our neighbor's yoke He means: the yoke which imprisons and torments our neighbor, whether near by or thousands of miles away; our neighbor, whom Jesus loves as much as He loves us, and then some, because Jesus has a godlike, overwhelming bias in favor of exploited Polish factory workers, tortured Salvadorian peasants, and our own guileless, defenseless children who will go up, with us, in a hell of flames unless we reverse and stop first the nuclear arms race and then the habit of war itself.

And if some of you are having a hard time with words like oppression, liberation, and—most of all—revolution, let me remind you that George Washington did not lead a conference or an excursion but a revolution. We are, as a nation, children of revolution. We used to be, as a nation, a beacon light for the oppressed and, frequently, their ally in revolutionary struggle. I suggest that what we are now, as a nation—one of the world's two great bullies—bent upon mutual and global destruction, can be changed, and that, as Christians, we can play a creative, redemptive part in the change.

But first we have to rediscover who we are: as a nation, children of revolution; as Christians, stewards of a nonviolent, dynamite Gospel. Amen.

Comment: Christians and Revolution

Four out of the church's 24 elders went on the warpath as a result of "Christians and Revolution," though they had been getting restless for some time because I was not conducting the kind of "caretaker" ministry they expected of an interim pastor. It is true, an interim pastor has to walk a fine line between the "caretaker" model and the "innovator" model. Keeping things going while helping people through their grief over the loss of their pastor is very important. But so is making relevant course corrections and gaining acceptance for needed change. The four elders actually petitioned the Presbytery of Utah to remove me, but a special meeting of Session, chaired by the presbytery executive, upheld my ministry solidly.

As a result of this controversy, a minority of elders and others open to change emerged. Together we scored some small gains, for example, in starting a Church and World Committee of Session and in increasing the congregation's giving to the world mission of the church. But the gains were small and they did not last. The new pastor proved to be very much at home in the Reagan Eighties: an apolitical Fundamentalist for whom "revolution" was and would always be a naughty word.

GOD'S GIFT, OUR CHOICE

Context: God's Gift, Our Choice

This sermon, preached in the First Presbyterian Church of Salt Lake City on Easter Sunday, 1983, was born of 90 percent despair and 10 percent hope, though I gamely tried to camouflage my despair. It was the 36th year of the Cold War. The two nuclear giants were facing each other with an arsenal of weapons that would have sufficed to destroy all life on Earth a thousand times over. In 1962, under Kennedy and Khrushchev, Armageddon was narrowly avoided. Nixon signed SALT I in 1974 and Carter signed SALT II in 1979, but the self-imposed limits on the race were largely symbolic. And in 1979 we got a taste of the force we had unleashed on the world—in the disaster at Three Mile Island.

To its credit, the Presbyterian Church, USA had launched a well-focused Peacemaking Program in 1980, challenging congregations to help reduce the tension between our country and the USSR in a variety of ways, including "people to people" travel and exchange. The record, by 1983 showed approximately 10 percent of our churches enlisted in the program, at least to the extent of receiving a special Peacemaking Offering on Worldwide Communion Sunday. Another 10 percent were generating vehement opposition, while 80 percent went on doing business as usual.

I had attended conferences and done a lot of reading on the subject. I continued to make donations to peace groups, like the Friends Committee on Legislation. But Easter 1983, the year President Reagan started spending our tax dollars on Star Wars, was the first time I would devote an entire sermon to the arms race—at the most heavily attended service of the year—in the State of Utah, beneficiary of countless defense contracts.

I knew that most of my hearers would be on the defensive and that many would aggressively resent my "spoiling" their Easter. Who wants to be reminded of unimaginable destruction, of burning flesh, of contaminated ruins on Easter Sunday of all Sundays? In the presence of hordes of children barely gathered from their Easter egg hunt?

I chose to stress life over death, an appropriate Easter emphasis. Will that newborn baby, greeted by a rosebud in church, be able to live out his natural life span or be cremated in a nuclear holocaust? It is up to us. God has set before us life and death and, through Moses, challenged us to "choose life." (Deut. 30:19—a basic text of the small Christian peace movement)

To buttress my plea, I quoted at length from an article in the Presbyterian magazine, *A. D.*, in which Professor Bruce Rigdon of our own McCormick Theological Seminary in Chicago tells about his uplifting Easter experience in Moscow. There were indeed only 18 million Communist party members in the USSR against 60 million Christians. Could we, as fellow-Christians, face incinerating them?

GOD'S GIFT, OUR CHOICE

By John R. Bodo
Interim Minister
First Presbyterian Church
Salt Lake City, Utah
April 3, 1983

OLD TESTAMENT: DEUTERONOMY 30:15–30
NEW TESTAMENT: LUKE 24:1–7

I do wish you a HAPPY EASTER! The chancel is covered with Easter lillies, symbols of new life. Among them there is a rosebud, symbol of a specific new life, heralding the birth of a baby boy. The sanctuary has been awash with glorious Easter music affirming God's gift of life and of new life for all who share the open secret of our Lord's resurrection. And next week we shall formally begin our participation in Presbytery's New Church Development Fund, which both demonstrates and promises new life for the small but growing Presbyterian community in Utah. All these symbols, events, and promises amount to a rousing agreement with the angel's rhetorical question, "WHY DO YOU SEEK THE LIVING AMONG THE DEAD?" Yes, this is the day of all days to affirm LIFE by enjoying a happy, thankful Easter.

But for anyone who is not a total OSTRICH, Easter 1983 cannot be simply unthinkingly happy. We all know that this is an Easter overcast by black clouds of fear because of the increasing THREAT TO LIFE, under which we live. We look at that rosebud and we wonder: will this little boy be permitted to live out his natural life? Will he, and millions like him, even reach school age? Or nursery school age? Anxiety in the face of an imagined threat is, no doubt, morbid. But anxiety in the face of a real threat is death-defying and life-affirming. Instead of clashing with the spirit of Easter, such anxiety seeks out the responsibilities, which the ever-fresh news of Easter lays upon us.

Some 22 years ago, at the time of the Cuban missile crisis, I read Nevil Shute's book, *On the Beach.* I am sure that many of you read it and many more saw the film. A nuclear exchange has destroyed the entire Northern Hemisphere. In Australia, people are waiting for the fallout to arrive and claim their lives. Meanwhile they are picking up a wondrously hopeful radio signal from somewhere in devastated North America. Marshaling the single submarine that is still seaworthy, they track down the signal, a fluke, in Seattle—a lifeless but eerily intact Seattle. They return to Australia and join others in dying with dignity, thanks to government-supplied pills.

When I finished the book, I sat down and wrote a few paragraphs which then stayed in a file until today—unpublished, unused, but not forgotten. I would like to share with you what I wrote some 22 years ago, when my daughters were about 8 and 6 and, of course, my little grandson was years from being born.

"No book I have ever read has made death more vivid, more anxiously personal for me than Nevil Shute's *On the Beach.* I have not seen the movie, and I do not wish to see it. I do not want the faces of Gregory Peck and Ava Gardner to superimpose themselves upon the completely individual, completely universal faces of Dwight and Moira.

Reading *On the Beach* has brought it home to me with awesome force how dependent we are on the PROPS, the TWO props, which sustain our courage to live in the face of inevitable death. As a specialist in religion, a 'professional Christian,' I have been dealing with one of these props, the hope of life after death, all my adult life. I have comforted others, and been comforted myself, with the incredible but incredibly comforting Gospel about the MAN who was more than a man, because He died but did not remain dead, and Who, by being raised from death, has left me—and other mortals like me—a bright ray of hope with which to light the black, threatening void.

But in concentrating upon this prop, I have been largely unaware of my dependence on THE OTHER PROP, which is the assumption, indeed the assurance, that when I die human life will go on, including the life of those persons in whom my own life has been invested and who have given my life most of its meaning.

It is a commonplace, I am sure, that the thought of the death of our loved ones is more intolerable than the thought of our own death. I should have known this. I did know it, in my head. But *On the Beach* made me feel it with wrenching pain, especially in the scene where the young wife learns that she will have to take the life of her baby before making her own exit, with her husband.

But my greatest surprise came in discovering how deeply I cared about the survival of the human race! I used to think that I should not, need not, care about this world after I am no more. I do not believe in spiritualism, in any form of contact between the dead and the living. Why, then, should I care? Why should I not say, with the French, '*après moi le déluge,*' ('after me, the flood')?

But reading *On the Beach* forced me to admit that I do care, desperately, about the survival of mankind. I can no longer be philosophical about dying thanks to the Easter hope, concerned only that all insurance premiums are paid up and that there is left, for my loved ones, enough to carry on. No, for the first time in my life I am compelled to admit that I need the other prop, too: the assurance that the human race will go on. Thanks to *On the Beach,* I have learned what I should have known all along: that 'no man is an island, entire of himself'; that I am 'involved in mankind'; and that PEACE, the only remaining alternative to an Earth without life, is my business, too. . . ."

Now let the scene shift rather abruptly. In the current issue of our Presbyterian monthly, *A. D.,* there is an article by Dr. Bruce Rigdon, professor of church history at McCormick Theological Seminary in Chicago. "Tell them the Church is Alive," is the title, and it is a first-person narrative of a recent visit to an Easter service in the Orthodox Cathedral in Moscow.

On the Saturday before Easter, in the evening, Dr. Rigdon inquires at the Intourist desk in his hotel about the way to the cathedral. "Sorry, it is a museum," the clerk tells him; "and all museums close at 5:00 o'clock." Undeterred, Rigdon boards the subway and arrives to find the cathedral packed and the square filled with additional thousands of Christians seeking entrance. Thanks to his American overcoat and clerical collar, he is shoehorned into the cathedral.

Eastern Orthodox churches have no seats. Worshipers do not mind standing, least of all at Easter, though the service turns out to run for SIX HOURS. It begins with the funeral of Jesus, around a casket covered with a cloth which shows the embroidered outline of the body of our Lord. At midnight, the cathedral empties. Worshipers join the other thousands outside to walk around the block, around the church, three times. It is the walk of the women to the tomb. Back at the cathedral, the patriarch of the Russian Orthodox Church bangs on the great gate three times with his staff. "We have come to care for the body of Jesus."

The door opens and the choir responds: "He is not here. He has risen from the dead, trampling down death by His death, and bestowing life to those in the tombs. Alleluia!" As he re-enters the cathedral, held up by the crowd, Rigdon is given a candle, as are all worshipers. In a few moments the cathedral, from which all the black has disappeared, is a sea of light. The music has become fast and joyous. The service moves on, through the last four hours, concluding with a celebration of the Lord's Supper, a victory banquet with the Risen Christ.

At 4:00 a.m., worshipers leave with all the special food they have brought to be consecrated. Every stranger in the congregation is invited to a home for a marvelous Easter breakfast. Rigdon finds himself taken under the wings of a family named, by extraordinary coincidence, VOSKRENENIA, "resurrection." Much later in the morning, when Rigdon has to leave, more than slightly stuffed, Mrs. Voskrenenia embraces her American guest and posts a message with him. "When you reach America again, tell them first from us, 'Christ is risen.' Tell them that here we are full of joy and love, that we are not afraid. Tell them that our life, the life of the Church, is a miracle. Tell them that the Church is alive. . . . and tell them that we must pray for each other and for the peace of the whole world."

There are fewer than 18 million Communists in Russia. There are over 60 million Christians.[1] They are our brothers and sisters in the Risen Christ.

1. *U.S. News & World Report,* August 2, 1982, p. 37.

What can we do to affirm God's gift of life—and of new life in Jesus Christ—on this day of all days, together with our brothers and sisters in Moscow, and everywhere in the Soviet Union, and everywhere in the world? How can we help lift the black cloud of fear which hangs over all of us, because of the blindness, the self-seeking, the insane stubbornness of the powers-that-be? What can we do for PEACE in the nuclear age, where peace is the only remaining alternative to global suicide?

The words we heard from Deuteronomy 30, the words of Moses, were addressed to a different people and in a wholly different situation, but they do have a prophetic ring and relevance.

> See, I have set before you this day life and good, death and evil. If you obey the commandments of the Lord your God . . . you shall live and multiply, and the Lord your God will bless you. . . . But if your heart turns away, and you will not hear, but are drawn away to worship other gods and serve them, I declare to you this day that you shall perish. . . . I call heaven and earth to witness against you this day, that I have set before you life and death, blessing and curse; therefore CHOOSE LIFE, that you and your descendants may live. . . .

Yes, life is a gift from God. New life, life even beyond death, is the supreme gift of God. But, like any gift, it can be accepted or rejected. We have a CHOICE. We have THE choice. The choice may not seem as stark as the words of Moses depict it. We do not see ourselves as angels or devils, agents of Satan or of God, in the struggle for mankind's survival. But the choice is stark: we either do SOMETHING for peace, and for justice without which peace cannot last; or, by doing NOTHING, we acquiesce in the Cold War whose outcome can only be one thing: the end of five thousand years of divine grace and human growth and, most likely, a lifeless planet. . . .

But we CAN choose LIFE! And the first thing we can do in casting a vote for life, for mankind, is exactly what we are doing now: CELEBRATE EASTER! Any authentic Easter service, whether here or in Moscow, is a protest vote, a symbolic act of defiance. Whose victory are we celebrating? The victory of Jesus Christ, who knows nothing about NATIONS but cares infinitely about PEOPLE, about PERSONS; Jesus Christ, whose church is mandated to side with the poor and challenge the mighty in the name of justice; Jesus Christ, the non-violent Prince of Peace, who taught us to love our enemies and forgave those who were driving nails into his hands and feet—and whom the tomb could not hold! Yes, the first thing we can do to let it be known that we are choosing LIFE is to celebrate this marvelous victory, the Crucified's Resurrection, which puts to flight all false gods—nationalism, communism, capitalism—on behalf of the one true God who gave us life and who would have us live, all of us, in peace and thanksgiving and love!

Of course, there are many other things we can do—many other first steps we can take—toward peace and life.

As members of the Session, we are to have a chance very soon to acquaint ourselves with our church's three-year-old Peacemaking program—a program committed to reversing the nuclear arms race but in no way limited to that objective.

As members of this congregation, we can attend the study group for adults on "Peacemaking in a War-Making World," which starts just two weeks from today. Some of the facts presented and discussed there may be hard to face, but there is far more hope in facing the facts than in hiding from them. Self-made shelters from reality are as treacherous as air raid shelters that are supposed to shield us from nuclear attack.

As individual Christians, we may join any one of several citizens organizations working for peace right here in Salt Lake City—some affiliates of national bodies, other purely Utahn. Of course, all the money, all the media, all the power are with the war-makers. But it is the peacemakers Jesus blessed; and all the organizations devoted to the pursuit of peace are crying for help. So anyone who says, "There is nothing I can do," has just not begun to look around. . . .

So, once again, I wish you a very HAPPY EASTER! You and I are in on the open secret of the Resurrection. We know that God will have the last word, because He had the next-to-the-last word on Calvary and the last word out of the empty tomb. That is our glad, thankful assurance. That, too, is the point at which our responsibilities as peacemakers begin. AMEN.

Comment: God's Gift, Our Choice

The people most disturbed by this sermon were again the ones who, a couple of months earlier, had complained about my ministry to the presbytery. Insofar as presbytery, and the majority of Session, had supported me, these critics decided to leave me alone. I was already at the halfway mark of my interim. They reasoned that I would soon be history.

They proved right; in fact, I would leave after just nine months of service in order to be able to attend the Seventh Assembly of the World Council of Churches in Vancouver, B.C. Having served as an interpreter at the Council's Organizing Assembly at Amsterdam in 1948, I never lost interest in, or contact with, the organization. First Church, Salt Lake City, would in turn call a safely apolitical, conservative evangelical pastor.

But I believe that "God's Gift, Our Choice" did accomplish something, at least in the short run. A nucleus of elders and others came to the fore, enabling the formation of a Church and World Committee of Session. The lecture-and-discussion series, "Peacemaking in a War-Making World," showed a surprising attendance and even got some public notice for the church. Thanks to contacts made through the series, a few members of First Church joined a local peace group.

Could I preach this sermon in a church this coming Easter? The "Evil (Soviet) Empire" is gone, but there are still thousands of nuclear weapons around, and they are not all in our hands. The threat they pose to life on Earth is more diffuse but no less real. And who is protecting us and our children and their children from the unyielding destruction that lurks in that ghastly memento of the Cold War, nuclear waste?

THE AGONY AND THE IRONY

Context: The Agony and the Irony

St. John's Presbyterian Church, Berkeley, was my fifth interim pastorate. I spent a full year there, commuting from our San Rafael home across the Richmond Bridge. Beyond the departure of an able pastor who had spent twelve years at the helm, there were other staff problems and changes that demanded attention. But all these conflicts revolved around persons and personalities. In terms of moral and spiritual priorities, St. John's stood tall. The membership, though small, was genuinely inclusive. The church plant was used extensively by community organizations. The church participated in a city-wide ministry with the homeless. More controversially, St. John's was a "sanctuary church" for refugees from Central America threatened with deportation by the Immigration and Naturalization Service. No subject was barred from discussion, whether from the pulpit or in church forums.

I wrote "The Agony and the Irony" for Martin Luther King's birthday which, 16 years after Dr. King's assassination, had been proclaimed a national holiday. The title is indebted, for no particular reason, to Irving Stone's novel about Michelangelo, *The Agony and the Ecstasy.* I would take the back seat to none in my admiration for Dr. King, but it did strike me as cruelly ironic how people, who had viciously opposed him or at least shown total indifference toward his fight for civil rights, were climbing on the birthday bandwagon.

The relevance of Jesus' indictment of the Scribes, the Pharisees (Matthew 23:29–20) is painfully obvious:

> Woe to you, Scribes and Pharisees, hypocrites! for you build the tombs of the prophets and adorn the monuments of the righteous, saying, "If we had lived in the days of our fathers, we would not have taken part with them in shedding the blood of the prophets!"

In St. John's Church, it was not necessary to prepare the congregation in any special way for "The Agony and the Irony," which would have been a "bombshell" in most other Presbyterian congregations. The purpose of this sermon was not to confront the members with a vision opposed to theirs but to confirm them in a shared commitment: to help the agony of Dr. King keep its prophetic edge in spite of the irony of his post-mortem official popularity. I did just one special thing by way of preparation: I composed for use in the service, "A Litany of Thanksgiving for America's Peaceful Freedom Fighters," reprinted after this sermon.

THE AGONY AND THE IRONY

By John R. Bodo
Interim Pastor
St. John's Presbyterian Church
Berkeley, California
January 15, 1984

SCRIPTURE: MATTHEW 23:29–39

Well, here we are just sixteen years after Martin Luther King's murder, celebrating his birthday as a national holiday! I have been trying to rejoice in this amazing development. I keep telling myself that we have come a long way in civil rights, thanks in large part to Dr. King's leadership and martyrdom. And I take the back seat to no one in my admiration of Dr. King's person and public ministry.

But my joy is spoiled, or at least sobered, by a pervasive sense of irony. A mere sixteen years have passed since Dr. King's murder, and everybody is acting as if he or she had been a member of the Southern Christian Leadership Conference or otherwise in the forefront of the civil rights struggle! Heads of business firms who would not employ a black person above the level of janitor or maid, bankers and realtors who would not allow black families to live anywhere except in their assigned ghettoes, service club stalwarts who fumed they would quit rather than admit "Negroes" to their clubs: all have not only survived the changes wrought by the Civil Rights Movement but are marching in the "Martin Luther King, Jr. Birthday Parade"—utterly forgetful of how they had personally aggravated Dr. King's agony, whether by actively impeding the Movement, or, more likely, by just looking the other way. . . .

WOE TO YOU . . .!

In what we number as the 23rd Chapter of his Gospel, Matthew collects all the "Woes" Jesus uttered against the Scribes and the Pharisees. The Evangelist arranges them in artful, purposeful sequence, from the general to the specific, from the lesser to the greater. The seventh and last "Woe" is also the gravest:

> Woe to you, Scribes and Pharisees, hypocrites! For you build tombs for the prophets, you adorn monuments for the righteous, and you say, "If we had lived in the days of our fathers, we would not have taken part with them in the shedding of the prophets' blood." Thus you witness against yourselves—that you are sons indeed of those who murdered the prophets. . . .

Then Jesus cries out in deepest distress: "O Jerusalem, killing the prophets and stoning those who are sent to you!"

According to Matthew's timetable, Jesus spoke these words a very short time before His own arrest, trial, and crucifixion. Thus His sorrow was not merely retrospective, historic: it was personal. Jesus was already grieving for Himself. His agony had begun long before the first lash of the whip or the first hammer blow on the first nail. He knew, because He knew both history and human nature, that some of the children of the very people who were about to kill Him, or at least let Him die, with total unconcern, would be clucking their tongues in disapproval of their fathers' shortsightedness and cruelty, echoing once again the smug refrain of hind-sight righteousness: "If we had lived in the days of our fathers, we would not have taken part with them in shedding the blood of the prophets!" Yes, the posthumous popularity of murdered prophets has always been high—and it is still high, as per our making the birthday of Martin Luther King a national holiday only sixteen years after his assassination.

SO WHO IS NEXT?

On this birthday of Dr. King, then, it may not be improper to ask: "So who is next?" What recently murdered witness to freedom, peace, or justice will be next to achieve national canonization of this ironic sort? A few currently erected "memorials" come to mind.

There is, for one thing, the Washington monument to the Vietnam War dead. It does not quite fit, because the men and women who died in Vietnam were victims rather than prophets: victims of bipartisan ineptness, stubbornness, and overbearing nationalism. But it does fit, in a way, because it does say, by its very existence, "If we had been the decision-makers at the time, we would have avoided the Vietnam agony." And that assumption partakes of the very irony we are talking about!

There is also the tribute paid to Richard Oakes in a TV ballet and to Karen Silkwood in a major film. Two little people—a Native American leader remembered, if at all, from the occupation of Alcatraz Island; and a factory worker with a sudden sense of mission born of her own death sentence from radiation poisoning. Both were killed under suspicious circumstances yielding inconclusive evidence. Both point a prophetically accusing finger not only at their allegedly unknown killers, but at a nation which has hardly begun to atone for the rape of the people of this land and which is now threatening the life of the world with uranium, plutonium, and all the rest—whether packaged for intentional destruction or inviting lethal accidents, because of the impossibility of safe production and safe disposal of wastes.

For my part, I would nominate for our next national holiday the four Catholic nuns murdered in El Salvador by our esteemed allies. Nothing ambiguous about their martyrdom! They were there to help the poorest of the poor—teaching them how to help themselves. Nonviolent, full of compassion, they presented an intolerable challenge to entrenched greed and power—just as their master had done nineteen centuries ago. To this day, their killers are unpunished while our government continues to finance and to supply weapons to their government. But I can just see a monument rising to their memory, the irony to crown their agony, some sixteen years from now. . . .

"WHEN WILL WE EVER LEARN?"

One of Pete Seeger's haunting antiwar songs includes the refrain, "when will they ever learn?" The answer to that question is "Never!" They will never learn. The old men who wage the wars in which they themselves seldom die will never learn. The "merchants of death" who sell arms right and left to Right or Left will never learn. The military careerists for whom a world at peace is a specter of unemployment and emasculation will never learn. None of these will ever learn unless they are first stripped of the power to work their mischief.

But if we put the question to ourselves, as Christians, it brings us right back to our text. The Scribes and Pharisees, the cream of the Hebrew crop in Jesus' day, were too cocky and smug to admit that they were truly sons of their fathers and that, if they had been around in their fathers' time, they would have persecuted and murdered God's prophets just as viciously, just as cruelly, as their fathers did.

But are we any different from them? We are the cream of today's Christian crop—educated and well-modulated, compassionate but never passionate (because that is poor manners), benevolent but uninvolved.

Pete Seeger's song is haunting, but there is a spiritual far more haunting still. Of course, the way we usually sing it, "Where you there when they crucified my Lord?" we make it sentimental and safe. But that song is meant to make us "tremble, tremble, tremble," because what it really asks is "Were YOU there?"

Are you able to answer that question honestly by saying, "Yes, Lord, I was there, but I am pretty sure I was not one of your Disciples, even though they did not do themselves proud, either. I was probably one of the Scribes or Pharisees, in the cheering section on Palm Sunday and in the lynch mob on Good Friday. I was also Caiaphas, proud of myself for safeguarding national security at the price of just one, paltry life; Pontius Pilate nipping a phantom revolution in the bud; and the Roman soldier driving the nails through Your hands, wincing at Your pain, mumbling to You 'Sorry, old chap! nothing personal. Just carrying out orders.' "

If we are able to answer the spiritual's "Were YOU there?" in this way, then we may also be able to celebrate Martin Luther King's birthday without adding irony to his agony. Amen.

A LITANY OF THANKSGIVING FOR AMERICA'S PEACEFUL FREEDOM FIGHTERS

Liturgist: Ruler of the nations, we thank You for men and women in our nation's past who fought, bravely and without bloodshed, for many kinds of freedom.

People: THEY KNEW THAT FREEDOM IS INDIVISIBLE, AND THAT FREEDOM FOR SOME DEMANDS FREEDOM FOR ALL.

Liturgist: We thank you for *John Woloman* and his fellow-Quakers who freed their slaves without approval from anyone except You.

People: WE THANK YOU FOR *HARRIET BEECHER STOWE* WHO, BY KINDLING COMPASSION FOR "UNCLE TOM," SET A NATION'S CONSCIENCE ON EDGE.

Liturgist: We thank you *W. E. B. Dubois* who first pointed out the fallacy of "separate but equal";

People: AND, TODAY OF ALL DAYS, FOR *MARTIN LUTHER KING* WHO GAVE HIS LIFE FOR THE DREAM OF "BLACK AND WHITE TOGETHER."

Liturgist: We praise you, Father, for *forgotten loners* who strove, against brutal odds, to secure the first rights for workers in industry;

People: AND FOR GREAT LEADERS OF LABOR—LIKE *SAMUEL GOMPERS, JOHN L. LEWIS, WALTER REUTHER*—WHO WERE ABLE TO BUILD UPON THEIR VISION AND BLOODY SACRIFICES.

Liturgist: We give you thanks, Father, for *Horace Mann* who fought the good fight to insure a basic education for every child, regardless of caste;

People: AND FOR *JOHN DEWEY* WHO SAW CHILDREN NOT AS COMPUTERS TO BE PROGRAMMED BUT AS YOUNG PERSONS TO BE HELPED TO GROW.

Liturgist: We praise You, O God, for the pioneers in the struggle for the liberation of women: for *Susan B. Anthony, Elizabeth Cady Stanton* and others;

People: AND FOR THE SINGLE-MINDED DEVOTION OF *MARGARET SANGER* WHO SPENT HERSELF WORKING FOR THE DAY WHEN EVERY CHILD WOULD BE A WANTED CHILD.

Liturgist: We thank You, Righteous Lord, for journalists like *Lincoln Steffens,* artists like *Thomas Nast,* novelists like *Upton Sinclair.*

People: THEY WERE SCORNED AS "MUCKRAKERS," BUT THEIR DISCLOSURES TOPPLED CORRUPT GOVERNMENTS, SPARKED REFORM, AND BROUGHT A SAFER, HAPPIER LIFE TO MILLIONS OF YOUR LITTLE PEOPLE.

Liturgist: We praise You, O God, for *Christians* who loved You enough to realize that others might love You differently but just as well.

People: CHRISTIANS LIKE *ROGER WILLIAMS,* WHO STRUCK THE FIRST PEACEFUL BLOW FOR RELIGIOUS FREEDOM, OR *WILLIAM PENN,* WHO CREATED A COMMONWEALTH WHERE EVEN NON-CHRISTIANS COULD DWELL IN PEACE.

Liturgist: We thank You, Father, for *missionaries* who chose to live among Indians, slaves, or alien immigrants. because they wanted to bring them into the mainstream of our society.

People: AND WE PRAISE YOU FOR *JOHN R. MOTT, JOHN A. MACKAY,* AND OTHER ECUMENICAL GIANTS WHO SET CHURCHES FREE FROM THE SHACKLES OF SELF-RIGHTEOUS SECTARIANISM AND HELPED US TO DISCOVER OUR UNITY IN "JESUS CHRIST, THE LIFE OF THE WORLD."

Liturgist: For all these great women and men, haunted, hounded and hunted in their day by people just like us, we thank You, O God;

People: AND WE PRAY FOR *WISDOM* TO DETECT TODAY'S PROPHETS AND FREEDOM FIGHTERS IN OUR MIDST: AND FOR *COURAGE* TO TAKE OUR PLACES ALONGSIDE THEM IN TODAY'S STRUGGLES FOR FREEDOM AND JUSTICE, MERCY AND PEACE. IN THE NAME OF JESUS CHRIST, OUR MASTER AND REDEEMER. AMEN.

Comment: The Agony and the Irony

Predictably, the sermon was well received. Several people expressed appreciation for the biblical perspective it gave them on the canonization of murdered (or ignored) prophets. My service as interim pastor came to an end when the church called a young man, a graduate of Union Theological Seminary, New York, my own *alma mater* (1942). The Rev. Tom McKnight has been pastor of St. John's, Berkeley, ever since, helping the congregation maintain its concern with social justice issues while being, for its own members and neighborhood, a compassionately caring community.

A LEVITE FOR A PRIEST

Context: A Levite for a Priest

I preached "A Levite for a Priest" on June 30, 1985, at the Immanuel Presbyterian Church of Tacoma, Washington, on the last Sunday of my service as interim pastor of that church. It was also my swan song as an *active* minister of the Presbyterian Church, USA. My *retirement* would begin the following day. Symbolically at least, I was closing a 43-year chapter of my life: ordained in 1942, retired in 1985. It was natural that I should want to say something that would summarize, perhaps even justify, my ministry.

For my sermon, I went back to a meditation it had been my honor to present at our church's 1958 General Assembly in Pittsburgh. I was still pastor of the First (now Nassau) Presbyterian Church of Princeton. It was my first time as commissioner (i.e., elected delegate) to a General Assembly; the honor would never be mine again. The meditation was entitled "Preacher, Stick to the Gospel!" *Presbyterian Life* published it in its September 1, 1958, issue.

"A Levite for a Priest" is an expansion of "Preacher, Stick to the Gospel!" based on the same biblical texts, making the same statement. Micah, a rich farmer in early Israel, living in an age of both religious and political confusion, engages a rootless young Levite as his live-in, private priest. He gets him cheap, sets him up properly with a shrine and a pulpit gown. Then, as the young priest begins his services, Micah mumbles to himself, delighted: "Now I know that the Lord will prosper me, because I have a Levite for a priest!"

What follows, both in the General Assembly meditation and, in expanded form, in the sermon is an affirmation of my lifelong conviction that, as preachers, we are indeed expected to "stick to the *Gospel*," but to the *whole* Gospel, *personal and social.* If we play it safe, contenting ourselves with the "personal" Gospel, with the prayer life, the family life, and maybe the afterlife, we risk becoming uncritical Levites to the Micahs, the powers-that-be of this world—prophets on the payroll whose main concern is to stay on the payroll.

A LEVITE FOR A PRIEST

By John R. Bodo
Interim Pastor
Immanuel Presbyterian Church
Tacoma, Washington
June 30, 1985

SCRIPTURE: JUDGES 17:1–13
LUKE 4:16–21

This sermon is based on the 17th chapter of the Book of Judges. In a composite translation, it reads as follows:

> There was a man in the hill country of Ephraim, whose name was Micah.
>
> Micah said to his mother, "You remember the 1,100 pieces of silver which were taken from you, and how you called down a curse on the thief, in my hearing? I have the money. I took it, and now I will give it back to you."
>
> His mother said, "May the Lord bless you, my son!"
>
> So Micah gave the 1,100 pieces of silver back to his mother who said, "I now solemnly dedicate this money of mine to the Lord for the benefit of my son—to make a carved idol and a cast image."
>
> Micah returned the money to his mother who took 200 pieces of silver and handed them to the silversmith who made them into an idol and an image, which stood in Micah's house.
>
> And Micah built himself a shrine, and he had a priestly robe and a set of household gods; and he installed one of his sons who became his priest. For in those days there was no king in Israel: every man did what was right in his own eyes.
>
> Now there was a young man of Bethlehem in Judah, of the family of Judah, who was a Levite; and he was living in Judah. This young man departed from Bethlehem to find a living wherever he could; and, as he journeyed, he came to the hill country of Ephraim, to the house of Micah.
>
> Micah said to the young man,"Where do you come from?"
>
> The young man said, "I am a Levite from Bethlehem in Judah, and I am going wherever I may find a place for myself."
>
> Micah said to him, "Stay with me, and be to me a father and a priest; and I will give you ten pieces of silver a year, and a suit of apparel, and your living."

> And the Levite was content to dwell with Micah, and he became like one of Micah's own sons. Micah installed the young Levite and he became Micah's priest and lived in Micah's house.
>
> Then Micah said, "Now I know that the Lord will prosper me, because I have a Levite for a priest. . . ."

From the distant and uncouth period of Israel's Judges, there comes to us a story full of food for thought: the story of Micah and the Levite.

Micah, no relation to the prophet, was a rich farmer who lived in an age similar to the long-ago "good old days" of our nation. There was no government to speak of. There were no taxes. Free enterprise ruled unhampered by such nuisances as labor unions, Medicare, or civil rights laws. "Every man did what was right in his own eyes." How much closer can you get to the WASP version, the White Anglo-Saxon Protestant version, of an American Garden of Eden?

Micah's morality was not exactly lofty. He had stolen 1,100 shekels, which his mother had saved up. Eventually his conscience or, more likely, the fear of Mom's curse, prevailed on Micah to return the money to her. But Micah was a very religious fellow, and a very religious fellow can afford to be a little lenient with himself—as long as he is good to his gods, keeping them safely by his side—and on his side. . . .

And Micah practiced his religion with a flourish. He did not need to keep his gods in the house, on a shelf. No, Micah could afford a special shrine for his gods, in a separate structure at the far end of the yard, where he could go and worship them on the Sabbath and on other holy days. In that way, Micah never had to mix business, or politics, with religion.

But Micah had one great sorrow: he did not have a minister for his private church. The gods, the teraphim, were there—in full array. The ephod, the priestly robe, hung neatly on the wall. But there was no one to wear it! In the absence of a proper minister, Micah had "ordained" one of his own sons as interim minister, but that arrangement seemed a bit incestuous even to his rugged individualism. Se he grumbled and hoped.

Then, suddenly, Providence smiled on Micah in the form of a Levite, a member of Israel's priestly caste, the equivalent of a Princeton graduate—at least! Micah did not waste any time. A practical man, he made a "godfather offer" to the Levite who, being just out of seminary, did not come very high. The very next Sabbath, Micah entered his private church for the first service of his private minister, beaming with contentment and muttering, "Now I know that the Lord will prosper me, because I have a Levite for a priest!"

The Levite, too, was something less than a hero. He did not have any money—a classic clergy predicament. As clergy, he was also slightly despised by the prosperous Micahs of the world because, while they could not get along without him, he could not get along without them—and they knew it, and he knew it.

But this young, Levite knew his "place." He knew that, in exchange for fulfilling his religious duties, he would be assured a comfortable livelihood—as long as he did not unduly antagonize his employer. Micah's offer was most acceptable to him. He knew the ancient Judean saying, "He who pays the piper calls the tune." In short, the young Levite was going to be a nice, safe minister. . . .

What does the story of Micah and the Levite have to say to us, American Christians, in the mid-1980s? Quite a bit.

These are tough and touchy times. Never before has our nation been richer or more powerful. Never before have we been so deeply frustrated and anxious. Why this strange paradox? One answer is that, for quite some time now, we have been facing problems which cannot be solved neatly, quickly, finally—and that we have not learned how to cope with such problems.

Remember the World War song, "Over There"? It reflected our traditional, cocky confidence at its purest. "We'll be over, we'll all be over, and we won't come back till it's over over there!" Yes, swift, drastic action: a dash of Yankee grit and smarts and the war would be won, the problem solved—just like that, bingo!

Well, this time it won't be over, neither over there nor over here. It won't be "over" in our lifetime. It won't be "over" in our children's lifetime, IF they are to have their lifetime. It will never again be "over" in that nice, final sense of a return to normalcy, to splendid isolation, with our self-serving, fairyland image of America about 100 years ago!

The energy crisis won't be over even if we got all the world's crude oil for ourselves at bargain rates. The consequences of our plunder of Planet Earth will keep us busy and floundering indefinitely.

The have-nots of the so-called Third World won't go away, no matter how many puppet regimes we support, no matter how many puppet goon squads we arm and train. Short of nuclear war, we cannot kill the peasants off fast enough—at the rate they multiply. We may have to think of something else!

The Soviet Union won't go away—short of nuclear war; in which case, in Mort Sahl's immortal words, "we'll all go together when we go." As a matter of fact, we depend on the Soviet Union, our "partner in peace-keeping"— just as the Soviet Union depends on us. The internal stability of the USSR depends on us cast in the role of "the enemy." Our own "more guns, less butter and, by all means, less bread for the poor" economy depends on the Soviet Union cast in the role of the enemy. Two huge, top-heavy, clumsy giants leaning on each other lest they fall in a heap!

And what we may call the "pluralism crisis" won't be over, either. Twenty-five million Blacks and millions of Non-Whites are here to stay as full-fledged Americans. Single persons, divorced persons, gay persons both female and male, are here to stay as full-fledged Americans; and if we do not make room for them in our churches and church programs, they will go on finding and founding other religious communities. And growing numbers of women insist on being not just full-fledged Americans but first-class human beings who happen to be female. The ERA and what it stands for can wait another three years, maybe, but not much longer.

So we have to go on living with problems both global and national, both public and intimate, which will not be "over"; problems which do not lend themselves to Lone Ranger solutions; problems which call for such scarce virtues as patience, tolerance, flexibility.

Yes, and self-criticism, self-criticism above all, the encouragement of self-criticism rather than its suppression. And this is where the story of Micah and the Levite speaks most eloquently to us.

For Christians are supposed to be, by God's own designs, critics of the existing order—whatever that order may be. As Christians, clergy or lay, we can never neatly divide humankind into white hats or black hats. As Christians, clergy or lay, we can never allow the manifest shortcomings of other systems to muzzle our critique of our own system. As Christians, lay or clergy, we are supposed to raise questions—tough-minded, critical questions: questions which are biblically informed but cannot be confined to the Bible, because God cannot be confined to the Bible.

Nor do we have to worry about having all the ANSWERS. When a group of Christians a few years ago tried to persuade Henry Kissinger to try a different tack in our foreign policy, the suave Secretary demurred. "Friends," he said, "you don't realize how complex this business is." Replied William Sloane Coffin: "Mr. Secretary, our responsibility is to insist that justice roll down like water and righteousness like a mighty stream. It is your business to figure out the proper plumbing!"

But these are tough and touchy times. The more frustrated and anxious we are as a nation about the stubborn complexity of the problems which beset us, the clearer the Micahs of this world are making it to the Levites that the tune of self-criticism is unwelcome and that, if the Levites value their pay and hope to keep on piping, they had better keep the music comforting and comfortable.

And too many present-day Christians, clergy and lay, are sons and daughters of that young Levite. They gladly restrict their "gospel" to the prayer life and the family life and maybe the afterlife, without ever touching upon any public issue. Or else, if they do comment on public issues, they copycat Jerry Falwell and the rest of the Immoral Minority: by sprinkling our military-industrial-governmental complex with holy water; by hailing the Contras, Somoza's wretched leavings, as freedom-fighters, while denying sanctuary to political refugees from Guatemala and El Salvador; by ignoring or treating with kid gloves the Nazi regime of South Africa which enjoys the blessing of its own Levites in the Dutch Reformed Church!

It is ironic how closely this viewpoint of our present-day Micahs resembles the religious policy of Communist dictatorships. Even the sternest Communist regime allows freedom of worship. People can pray all they want. They can shape their family life according to the dictates of their faith. And they can enjoy the hope of life after death unhampered. The only absolute restriction upon churches under tight-fisted Communist regimes is that they may not "meddle with politics." Translation: they may not criticize the government and/or the "power elite."

Yes, these are tough and touchy times, and, for the moment, our homegrown Micahs seem to have the whole scene to themselves, while the Levites either fawn on them, whether from pulpits or on the tube, or else keep piping the old, soothing tunes to keep the paychecks coming. Things look bad, yes; but I say there are signs of hope.

There is hope in the Sanctuary Movement. Over 200 churches have declared themselves, over 20 of them Presbyterian. And the power of the Movement's witness far exceeds its numbers.

There is hope in the great changes which are occurring in the Catholic Church, not only in Latin America but in the U. S. First the Bishops' Letter on peace. Now the Bishops' Letter on economic justice. The Catholic Church is not frozen in time!

There is hope, above all in God's unchanged commitment to the oppressed, the poor, the hungry, which a growing number of ministers and churches are beginning to understand and to work with. It used to be that American Christians would divide the Gospel into two parts: personal and social. The former was holy, the latter unholy—or at least suspect. In this way, we would divide ourselves into Liberals and Conservatives, or Evangelicals and Social Actionists. But today, thanks to God's unchanged commitment to the oppressed, the poor, the hungry, more and more Christians are awakening to the wholeness, the indivisible oneness of the Gospel as well as to the political causes of hunger, poverty, and oppression.

Yes, we have begun to realize that hunger is political: one little Act of Congress can feed (or starve) more people than we can feed with ten years' worth of gifts to the One Great Hour of Sharing!

We have begun to realize that racism is political. The government of South Africa survives because of our government's so-called "constructive engagement" policy, which translates into "benign neglect"—or "malign neglect."

And it must be obvious to us by now that war is political and that therefore peace is political. There are powerful persons and institutions—economic, military, governmental—whose self-interest dictates that we merely toy with peace while staying on a war footing, even if the risk of accidental global suicide increases with the manufacture of every nuclear weapon; and, at the last count, we were making them at the rate of three a day.

Yes, I am certain of God's unchanged commitment to the oppressed, the poor, the hungry—and of His wrath for people and systems that make them and keep them so. I am equally certain of the indivisible oneness of the Gospel, personal and social, and of the moral and spiritual imperative for Christians, lay and clergy, to become more informed and more active, more CRITICALLY informed and active, in the politics of hunger, racism, sexism, the Cold War, and all the rest!

When Jesus came to Nazareth to preach his first sermon in the most difficult church on earth, His home church, He chose as His text a prophecy of Isaiah (61:1–2) which was to set the tone for His entire ministry and then linger on, as a prod and a challenge for His followers, through the ages.

> The Spirit of the Lord is upon me, because He has anointed me to preach good news to the poor; He has sent me to proclaim release to captives and recovery of sight to the blind; to set at liberty those who are oppressed; to proclaim the acceptable year of the Lord.

Jesus was not much of a success in His ministry. The prosperous Micahs of His day rejected Him. So did their timid or fawning Levites.

He enlisted only twelve full-time Disciples but, when the crisis broke, one betrayed Him and eleven deserted Him.

Yes, Jesus was, of all the prophets, the most lonely because, more than any other prophet, He preached—and lived—the whole gospel: forgiveness to the penitent and judgment to the self-righteous; a new self-respect for the humble and a fierce warning to the high-and-mighty; precious promises to the downtrodden, and ruthless exposure for those who would cloak their self-interest, personal or corporate, in the respectable rags of religion.

The Micahs among us are saying the same old thing over and over: "Preacher, stick to the Gospel!" They mean a privatized gospel, a pie-in-the-sky gospel, or else a "bless-the-bomb" gospel, a "bless-big-business" gospel, a "bless-the-unborn-let-the-living-be-damned" gospel.

Jesus stuck to the Gospel, but He stuck to the whole Gospel. His faithfulness did not advance His career much. His career came to a quite abrupt end—on a cross. But then, just as abruptly, Jesus resumed His career—thanks to Someone who would not let Him stay dead, but rolled away that stone.

And this Jesus—"Prophet, Redeemer, Liberator"—is still at large. AMEN.

Comment: A Levite for a Priest

Any effect "Micah and the Levite" might have had on the Tacoma congregation was blunted or sidetracked by the fact that it was my last Sunday and that the people had prepared a lovely farewell party following the service. Immanuel was a small, friendly church, hard to challenge, because of a pervasive passivity. It is easier, I have found, to make a dent in a brick wall than in a foam rubber wall.

I would have liked to retire from a more exciting interim pastorate than was mine at Immanuel, Tacoma, but I was not ready to retire, anyway. Fortunately, there is no formal age limit on serving as interim pastor. As a matter of fact, if you are in fair health and have a good track record, age may be a factor in your favor.

Since my formal retirement in 1985 I have served four more interim pastorates: Westminster Presbyterian Church, Dayton, Ohio; First Presbyterian Church, Vallejo, California; Immanuel Presbyterian Church, Los Angeles; and First Presbyterian Church, Napa, California. God willing, I may be able to serve one or two more.

My commitment to the oneness, the wholeness of the Gospel has not changed and is not likely ever to change. "Preacher, stick to the Gospel!" or "A Levite for a Priest" remains a heartfelt summary, in sermon form, of what I hope my ministry has been all about. . . .

EPILOGUE

What are some of the conditions of faithful prophecy on the payroll?

First and foremost, we must deal with the biblical materials related to any public issue we feel called upon to treat. I respectfully disagree, however, with the oft-quoted dictum: "Where the Bible speaks, we speak; where the Bible is silent, we are silent." Of course we must take into account whatever the Bible has to say, explicitly, on the subject. But this does not mean that the Bible's words are "law." In fact, there are times when we may need to oppose what the Bible has to say. For example, the only guidance we find in Scripture on the problem of population is "Be fruitful and multiply. . . ." This was readily perceived to be God's will in a primitive, agrarian society, where children were needed in the fields and where they also constituted the only old-age insurance of their parents. But I cannot believe that uncontrolled multiplication is still God's will—on an overcrowded planet where five billion people are jostling one another and where half of them lie down hungry every night!

As for issues on which the Bible is silent, I propose that, if they significantly affect human life, we have to address them just the same in the light of the Gospel, the Good News that God was in Jesus sharing with us the full round of our life. There were no corporations, no contraceptives, no computers in biblical times. Does that mean that we are not supposed to offer any prophetic critique of the effects of these newcomers on the human scene? Or of dozens of other equally promising or threatening additions to our common life?

Faithful prophecy also requires that we study and enlist other resources, both religious and secular. In my denomination, the Presbyterian Church, USA, two recent creeds—the *Confession of 1967* and *A Brief Statement of*

Faith (1993)—offer valuable guidance. So do the occasional *Social Deliverances* of our General Assembly. These thoroughly researched comments on current public issues can be very helpful both for what they say and for the authority they carry. They are not papal encyclicals, but they do represent at least a majority vote of our church's highest governing body. Acceptance of a sermon on a controversial issue can be facilitated by reference to, or even advance distribution of, a General Assembly social deliverance on the subject. It can at least assure the congregation that their pastor is not a quixotic loner, but is reflecting the mind of the leadership of the church of which they are a part.

While social deliverances of the General Assembly are always drafted with the aid of lay experts on the issue, it is particularly desirable for the pastor to involve lay talent in the congregation. Suppose the issue under consideration is proposed changes in our system of welfare. Beyond reading at least several well-chosen newspaper and magazine articles, the pastor will be well-advised to consult with a small group of members: an economist, a social worker, and, by all means, a present or former welfare recipient. These same members, having participated in the drafting of the sermon, may then be willing to serve on a follow-up panel immediately after the service. To prevent unnecessary, destructive controversy, it is extremely important to offer the congregation an immediate opportunity to "talk back." The participation of fellow lay persons in such a session will help avoid undue focusing on the pastor's person by keeping people's minds on the issue.

Having prophesied on a controversial public issue, it is highly advisable to provide some action follow-up for members who responded positively to the sermon and would now like to do something about the issue. In churches of mainline denominations, it is essential to keep such follow-up suggestions on a strictly individual basis. Fundamentalist and independent congregations can act corporately, because their membership is homogeneous: the members belong because they agree with the doctrine, both religious and political, up to one hundred percent. Mainline congregations are broadly inclusive. Churchwide agreement cannot be taken for granted on any issue. Therefore it is important to avoid the very appearance of a collective commitment. On the other hand, it is safe and helpful to inform people what secular organizations they might explore and perhaps join, if they would like to become active, as individual citizens, on the issue. The success of the effort at housing integration in Princeton, New Jersey (see sermon, "Who Is My Neighbor," p. 26) was due in no small part to the creation of the Princeton Housing Group long before the sermon was preached, which made that group instantly available to any church members who, having signed the "Covenant of Open Occupancy," wanted to do something about desegregating the housing market.

A final condition for faithful prophecy on the payroll: when you preach on a controversial public issue, you will need to preach with *love* for your people, no matter how deeply involved they may be in the system or structure of injustice which you are about to indict in God's name. Denunciations alone will get you nowhere, except perhaps to the end of your tenure as pastor. People will not stand for being bawled out, least of all from the pulpit. Old-time revival preachers used to scold people and threaten them with hell, and it worked as long as people believed in hell and stood in awe of preachers. Those days are gone.

So we need to appeal in our preaching to what is best in our hearers: to their love for the Lord; to their sense of fair play; their compassion for the disadvantaged; their concern about their children and the kind of world they will be leaving for them. Such preaching will, of course, be in the first person *plural.* If I, in the role of prophet, feel untainted by the evil, uninvolved in the injustice with which I am about to confront my congregation, I need to remember—before I open my mouth—that I am on their payroll. And I must keep this in mind not just because I may be rightly worried about my job if I make them too nervous, but because, by the very fact that I am on their payroll, I am *one of them.* So the prescription is: love—in the first person plural.